# Sibelius
# and
# His Masonic Music

# Sibelius and His Masonic Music

## Sounds in 'Silence'

*Second Revised and Abbreviated Edition*

iUniverse, Inc.
New York  Bloomington  Shanghai

# Sibelius and His Masonic Music
## Sounds in 'Silence'

iUniverse books may be ordered through booksellers or by contacting:

iUniverse
1663 Liberty Drive
Bloomington, IN 47403
www.iuniverse.com
1-800-Authors (1-800-288-4677)

ISBN: 978-0-595-50088-8 (pbk)
ISBN: 978-0-595-61371-7 (ebk)

Printed in the United States of America

*Dedicated to the memory of*

*Marshall Kernochan*

*John Kernochan*

*Toivo Nekton*

*George Sjöblom*

*and*

*Paul Sjöblom*

*and with deep appreciation to*

*Roger Nekton*

*Neil Sjöblom*

*and*

*Steven Sjöblom*

# CONTENTS

# PREFACE TO
# THE FIRST EDITION

For the past several decades, members of the Grand Lodge, F. & A. M., of the State of New York, have felt both a special reverence for Sibelius's Masonic ritual music and a great pride in their Grand Lodge's role in disseminating this important work. The musical manuscript presented by the composer to the Grand Lodge serves the membership as a physical reminder of how the ideals of Freemasonry transcend national borders to unite individuals in fraternity.

As time has passed, however, knowledge has faded concerning the rich social and institutional fabric surrounding the apotheosis of Sibelius's composition. The contributions of men such as Marshall Kernochan, Charles Johnson, and Toivo Nekton have been forgotten.

Dr. Hermine Williams has performed a remarkable feat of reconstructing the details of the process through which Sibelius's Opus 113 was composed and made available to both Freemasons and the general public. Her tireless research on both sides of the Atlantic provides new insights into how Sibelius drew upon Freemasonry to express a pantheistic spirituality, but also illuminates the role that Freemasonry played in Finnish-American relations at the beginning of the twentieth century. Freemasons everywhere owe Dr. Williams a debt of gratitude for this significant contribution to Masonic musical scholarship.

*William Moore, Director*
*Livingston Masonic Library*
*New York, New York*
*January 1998*

# ACKNOWLEDGMENTS

In the spring of 1994, when library volunteers were sorting through the contents of one of the many boxes shipped from the Robert R. Livingston Masonic Library in New York City to its annex in Utica (NY), some handwritten pieces of music were uncovered, which seemed of little value until someone noticed that several pages bore the name of Jean Sibelius. Those volunteers were Charles Haskin, Frederick De La Fleur, and Robert O. Williams, and to them is owed a debt of gratitude by Sibelius scholars for their thoughtful preservation of what are now known to be very important documents. This material, brought to me for verification of its authenticity, included Sibelius's 1948 manuscript of opus 113, the original wrapping paper in which the manuscript was shipped from Järvenpää to New York, the proof sheets for the 1950 edition with Sibelius's (autograph) corrections, and related correspondence.

My research into Sibelius's association with Freemasonry and his writing of the Masonic ritual music has had the generous assistance of many individuals to whom I am extremely grateful. First and foremost, the 1998 edition of this book would never have been written had it not been for the enthusiastic interest and constant encouragement from Ilkka Kalliomaa. It was he who introduced me to the Finnish language, provided me with information about Freemasonry in Finland, put me in touch with Masons at Suomi Suur-Loosi, and procured for me *Sibeliuksen Rituaalimusiikki* by Einari Marvia, an indispensable source of information

William Moore, who was then Director of the Livingston Masonic Library, offered unlimited access to the Sibelius materials owned by the Grand Lodge of New York. He was most helpful in drawing my attention to requisite sources about Freemasonry, correcting errors of fact in the manuscript, and providing a constant measure of support for my book.

Fabian Dahlström, one of Finland's preeminent Sibelius scholars, went out of his way to give me every scrap of information he had or could discover concerning opus 113. This included sending me pages from a preliminary draft of his recently published catalogue of works by Sibelius and summarizing the contents of uncatalogued correspondence in the National Archives in Helsinki.

One of the greatest pleasures in researching material for this book was being able to share discoveries with John Marshall Kernochan—Nash Professor Emeritus of Law at Columbia University and son of Marshall Kernochan—who, after his father's death in 1955, assumed the position of president of Galaxy Music Corporation. He illumined the complex world of copyright law, provided copies of personal correspondence from Sibelius to his father, offered me continual advice, and shared his own personal remembrances of a visit to Järvenpää in 1939. Much of the material provided by John Kernochan was set forth in my 1999 supplement to the first edition of *Sibelius and His Masonic Music*. Sadly, John did not live to see this second edition in print. His death occurred 29 October 2007.

In the mid 1990s, a chance meeting with John G. Wright, a District Deputy Grand Master and member of the Masonic lodge in Geneva (NY), lead to my introduction to Neil and Steven Sjöblom. They are the grandsons of George (Yrjö) Sjöblom and have become the custodians of correspondence, photos, and printed materials related to Finnish-American cultural exchanges (1915–1971) that they inherited from their grandfather's estate. Included in this private collection are letters from Sibelius, Olin Downes, Marshall Kernochan, and A. Walter Kramer. Not only did Neil and Steven invite me to research this collection as often as needed, they also put me in touch with their uncle, Paul Sjöblom, in Helsinki. He, in turn, wrote me numerous letters and willingly answered my unending list of questions about his family and about his contacts with Sibelius and Wäinö Sola.

Many other individuals supplied articles, unpublished materials, and photos; helped with translations; and offered library assistance. Among them, the following are owed special thanks: Roger Nekton of Exeter, NH, who graciously made available correspondence and surviving documents related to his grandfather, Toivo Nekton, which were discussed in the 1999 supplement to the first edition of *Sibelius and His Masonic Music*; Einari Marvia of Helsinki; Kari Kilpeläinen, Dept. of Musicology, Helsinki University; Anne Alakallaanvaara of the Helsinki University Library; Marja Pojohla of the National Archives of Finland; Anna Krohn of the Sibelius Academy; Erin Davis, Rare Book and Special Collections Librarian, Irwin Library of Butler University, Indianapolis, IN; Joseph Nolte, Assistant Librarian, Iowa Masonic Library, Cedar Rapids, IA; Joan Wolek and the Burke Library staff of Hamilton College, Clinton, NY; Yrjö Hakkinen and Ilkka Runokangas of Suomi Suur-Loosi and Sakari Lehmuskallio of Suomi Loosi 1; Wallace McLeod, Executive Secretary of the Philalethes Society; Robert E. Freyer, Wanatagh Morton Lodge, North Belmore, NY; Steven Gerber, E. C. Schirmer, Boston, MA; Jussi Tarjamo and Eija Janinen of New York; and Neil Sjöblom and Marianita Amodio for photo reproductions that were used as illustrations in the first edition of this book.

Last, but not least, I wish to thank my husband, Jay Williams, for his continued patience and support during the researching and writing of the first edition of this book, the supplement to that edition, and this, the second revised and abbreviated edition.

Documents in the Sjöblom Family Collection, in the Nekton Family Collection, and in the possession of the John Kernochan family have been used with exclusive permission and may not be reproduced. Permission was granted to quote from *Ars Quatuor Coronatorum* by QCCC Ltd. and from Erik Tawaststjerna's *Sbelius* by Faber and Faber Ltd. Quotations from and reproductions of letters, manuscripts, photos, and other documents in the Robert Livingston Masonic Library, the archives of the Helsinki University Library, and the "Sibelius Family Collection 36/94" in the National Archives of Finland have been used with permission and may not be copied in any form.

*January, 2008*                                          *Hermine Weigel Williams*

# *PROLOGUE*

When Erik Tawaststjerna completed his study of Jean Sibelius in the late 1980s, it was anticipated that his multi-volume publication would become the definitive source for information about the life and music of Finland's most revered composer.[1] While there is no denying the musicological significance of Tawaststjerna's contribution, one nevertheless searches in vain among the pages of his monumental work for any discussion of Sibelius's association with Freemasonry and the music (opus 113) he composed for Masonic rituals.[2]

Why have biographers cloaked the Masonic aspect of Sibelius's career in secrecy? Why have they chosen to ignore a musical composition that was and continues to be of great importance to Masons in Finland and the United States? Is it because "the silence of Järvenpää" has become so much a part of the Sibelius portrait that no one dares to penetrate that silence? The answer would seem to be a resounding "yes!" as one writer after another claims nothing of any consequence came from the composer in the final thirty years of his life. Even as recently as 1995, one can read that between 1931 and 1938 Sibelius neither composed nor arranged anything "apart from the 8th [!]symphony and a minor choral arrangement in 1935." During this same period he also "did not publish anything, and after 1938 he just revised older works."[3]

---

1  Tawaststjerna's *Jean Sibelius* was first published in a Finnish edition (1965–88) and then in a Swedish edition (1991–93). In addition, two volumes of a three-volume abridged edition of Tawaststjerna's *Jean Sibelius*, prepared and translated into English by Robert Layton, were published by the University of California Press in 1976 and 1986; volume three was published by Faber & Faber in December of 1997.

2  In a letter to the author dated 13 October 1995, Einari Marvia indicated his disappointment that his friend "Erik Tawaststjerna did not write anything about Sibelius's ritual music in his biography," especially since "he had asked me to send him in all confidence my research about this music for this express purpose." Publication of Marvia's research (1972; 1984) was under the auspices of his Masonic lodge in Finland.

3  Kilpeläinen, "Sibelius Eight. What Happened to It?," 34.

In an attempt to rectify this inexplicable oversight of an important aspect of the composer's career, Einari Marvia (1915–97) researched the history of Sibelius's opus 113 and its relationship to Masonic activities in Finland. His study was scheduled for publication in 1972 as a commemorative volume for the 25th anniversary of the Grand Lodge of Finland (Suomi Suur-Loosi). Before completing his manuscript, Marvia sought information from the Grand Lodge of New York concerning their published editions of opus 113. In particular, he wanted to know if Sibelius received any royalties from the sale of the 1936 and 1950 editions.

Marvia's professional and fraternal credentials placed him in a unique position to undertake this research. As a musicologist and composer, he was well equipped to analyze the autograph manuscripts and sketches in the archives of the Sibelius Academy and Helsinki University. As a Mason, his fraternal membership allowed him direct access to documents in the possession of Suomi Suur-Loosi, including correspondence sent to Sibelius from the Grand Lodge of New York. It also gave him the ability to interpret those documents with respect to Masonic rituals. What he lacked were documents that he presumed were available in New York City, such as Sibelius's correspondence with Marshall Kernochan and Charles Johnson, among others. Unfortunately, the information Marvia sought could not be supplied by the Grand Lodge in New York and he therefore was placed in the awkward position of having to publish his book before getting answers to some important and intriguing questions. It was for this reason that the 1972 publication of his research was issued in a limited edition; he was confident that the information requested from New York would be forthcoming at a later date. Over the course of the following decade, Marvia uncovered enough new information about Sibelius's Masonic ritual music to warrant the publication of a revised edition of his book, *Sibeliuksen Rituaalimusiikki*, in 1984. At this time he also made available for those not conversant with the Finnish language a brief synopsis of his findings in English for distribution through the Grand Lodge of Finland.[4]

The present study of opus 113 owes a considerable debt to Einari Marvia for his pioneering efforts in shedding light on one of Sibelius's last compositions. Prior to Marvia's 1984 publication, information about opus 113 or about Sibelius's role as a Mason was, for the most part, limited to articles in Masonic publications. Often this information was either incomplete or incorrect, and

---

4    [Einari Marvia], "The Ritual Music of Sibelius," [typescript, 17pp.].

never did it offer the kind of in-depth analysis of the music that can be found in *Sibeliuksen Rituaalimusiikki*.[5]

Admittedly, the number of people who know the Finnish language well enough to make use of Marvia's research is relatively small. It therefore seemed appropriate to publish, in English, another study of this same subject, one that not only drew from research done by Marvia and other scholars, but also introduced new information based on recently discovered documents pertaining to the American editions of opus 113. This study was published as *Sibelius and His Masonic Music* in 1998. Soon after that book was published, a considerable number of documents came to light from the private papers of Marshall Kernochan and Toivo Nekton, owned respectively by their sons, John Kernochan and Roger Nekton. So important were these materials, it was deemed necessary to publish in 1999 a twenty-five page supplement to the 1998 book. Since many persons and libraries who purchased the 1998 hardcover book did not order the supplement, much valuable information continues to be hidden from view. To make this material accessible in a single volume, it was decided to issue a revised and abridged version of both the 1998 and 1999 publications.

This new edition of *Sibelius and His Masonic Music* incorporates an investigation into questions pertaining to copyright agreements and royalties, as set forth in the 1999 supplement mentioned above. Omitted from this new edition, however, is much of what was discussed in chapter nine of the 1998 book—a chapter that was devoted to an analysis, with musical examples, of each of the pieces that comprised the 1950 edition of Sibelius's Masonic music. Those interested in the compositional aspect of the music are advised to consult the 1998 edition of this study. Also omitted from this second edition are illustrations of sample pages from the 1950 manuscript that show the composer's editorial markings and photographs of the composer as well as other persons who were closely linked with the publication and performance of *Masonic Ritual Music*.

Those who have expressed an interest in discerning Sibelius's views of religion will find this study offers considerable information about that aspect of the composer's life. First and foremost, the texts chosen by the composer

---

5    Even fairly recently published studies about Sibelius continue to set forth incorrect information about the composer's role as a Mason and his ritual music. See, for example, Goss, ed., *The Sibelius Companion* (1996), 211–12, 273, 279n1, 386–8 and 411–12.

for opus 113 reveal his innermost feelings toward the unfathomable realm of the divine. Second, the attention paid by Sibelius to "Musique réligieuse"—in its many guises and over a period of time extending from the 1930s to the 1950s—underscores the fact that this opus was of paramount importance to him. Opus 113 brought forth the "sounds" of musical creativity in that period in the composer's life so often described as one of "silence."

# CHAPTER ONE

## "MUSIQUE RÉLIGIEUSE"

On 18 August 1922, the Grand Lodge of New York constituted Suomi Lodge No. 1 in Helsinki, thereby officially reintroducing Freemasonry to Finland after an absence of almost 100 years.[1] That date holds significance for both Finnish and American Masons because it marks the establishment of the "sole and only outpost of American Freemasonry on the old continent."[2]

After Finland declared its independence on 6 December 1917 following the October Revolution and succeeded in ending the civil war waged on its soil from 1918 to 1919, the country was at long last able to welcome the transforming spirit of democracy. A group of Masons, drawn from Finland's expatriates living in or near New York City and from Americans residing in Finland, felt the time was ripe for testing the new found freedoms that had come to the Finnish people. In June 1922, eight Masons formally petitioned the Grand Lodge of the State of New York for a warrant so that Freemasonry could be reestablished in their homeland. "Grand Lodge law provided that (1) a petition for the constitution of a new lodge must be signed by eight Master Masons in good standing and (2) such petition must be accompanied by a

---

1   Throughout the text, the abbreviations GLNY and SSL will be used to refer, respectively, to the Grand Lodge of New York and the Grand Lodge of Finland (Suomi Suur-Loosi). Suomi Lodge No. 1 refers to Suomi Loosi N:o 1 and is distinct from Suomi Suur-Loosi. Although the correct title of Sibelius's lodge should be Suomi Loosi 1 (i.e., omitting the abbreviation for "number"), the more commonly used title has been adopted for this book because that is the way the lodge was designated in correspondence and documents related to this study.
2   Nekton, "Highlights in the History of American Freemasonry in Finland 1922–1949," 26.

'waiver' or 'consent' of the nearest existing lodge."[3] The GLNY acted favorably upon their request and appointed Toivo Nekton, one of the expatriates, to be District Deputy, "for the Republic of Finland."

Prior to the 1822 ban on Freemasonry imposed by the Russian Czar, lodges in Finland had operated under the "continental system." Now, with their request to the GLNY for a restitution of Freemasonry, they initiated the possibility for the American system to become permanently established in continental Europe. Nekton was very conscious of the deep-seated relationship between the democratic system of Freemasonry that he was about to introduce to Finland and the founding of the Republic of Finland, which in and of itself was being patterned closely on the American system of government. The "continental system" of Freemasonry, which governed lodges in Finland from 1756 until 1822 had been "employed by its leaders" as a means for "monarchic power and aggrandizement."[4] It was for this reason that Czar Alexander I banned Freemasonry on 12 August 1822. He feared that Gustavus Adolphus IV of Sweden would use the offices and influence of Freemasonry to subvert and ultimately undermine his power over this newly acquired territory.

Before the American system of Freemasonry could be adopted by the Finns, its rites and rituals had to be translated from English into Finnish. This arduous and time-consuming task was willingly undertaken by Toivo Nekton. Not only did Nekton translate the materials used by the GLNY. He also guided the Masons in Finland in the correct implementation of the American system. He did this during several visits to Helsinki.

In anticipation of the constitution of Suomi Lodge No. 1, Finnish Masons who were considered charter members of the newly organized fraternity in Helsinki took it upon themselves to suggest names of other prominent Finnish citizens who should be invited to join the fraternity. Out of the more than eighty invitations issued and applications accepted, twenty-seven persons decided to enter into Masonic membership. They included Jean Sibelius, Ernst Linko (a musician), Sigurd Wettenhovi-Aspa (an artist), Axel Solitander (Consul General at New York), and Samuli Sario (a former Senator).[5]

---

3    Nekton, *Morton Lodge No. 63 F. & A. M.: Its History 1797–1947*, 11.
4    Nekton, "Highlights," 27.
5    According to Einari Marvia, in his *Sibeliuksen Rituaalimusiikki*, 9–10, it was Wettenhovi-Aspa who extended the initial invitation to Sibelius to apply for membership in the fraternity. Wettenhovi-Aspa painted several portraits of Sibelius.

A few days before Suomi Lodge No. 1 was officially constituted, the charter members met to discuss, among other things, what roles Wettenhovi-Aspa, Linko, and Sibelius would fulfill in the new organization. The records of that meeting indicate that Wettenhovi-Aspa was to be the fraternity's historian and write a history of the lodge, Linko was to serve as organist, and Sibelius was to provide music for the rituals.[6] In return for sharing their particular talents, the three were to have their fees waived for joining the fraternity and for the first year's membership. Of the three, only Linko immediately fulfilled his obligation.

In 1949 Nekton wrote an article that chronicled the special events connected with the re-establishment of Freemasonry in Finland. His eye-witness account describes how a delegation of five Americans from the GLNY, including the Grand Master, traveled to Helsinki to conduct the rites of constitution. They brought with them as gifts a beautifully bound Bible and a set of silver jewels. The twenty-seven people who were to become Masonic members on 18 August 1922 were initiated, passed, and raised in the three degrees on the same day. At the conclusion of those rites, a dinner was held to honor the American delegation who had made this occasion possible. Musical entertainment was provided by a thirty-piece orchestra, which played "a great deal of Sibeliana."[7]

Sibelius attended the dinner but, "true to his habitual reserve," he did not enter into much conversation until coffee was served. It was then that Sibelius, who was seated opposite Nekton, leaned forward and in Finnish asked: "How is it possible that we may sit here and enjoy ourselves so festively after the solemnities of this day?"[8] Obviously Sibelius had not entered into the day's events light-heartedly. It was, after all, a very emotional time for someone who at the age of 57 had personally experienced the rough and rocky road that led up to those festivities. From the turn of the century onward, Sibelius had dared to support events that championed nationalism and freedom for the people of Finland. Now he was actively participating in a dream that had become reality.

Although Nekton spent the winter of 1922 in the United States, he did not lose contact with members of Suomi Lodge No. 1. Among those with whom he corresponded was Sibelius and, as his extant letters and visits with the

6    These records are in the archives of SSL.
7    Nekton, "Highlights," 24.
8    Ibid., 25.

composer prove, a very close relationship developed between them. Included in their initial correspondence was a request from Sibelius for help in having several of his works issued by the firm of Carl Fischer, an American publisher. How much credit is due Nekton for negotiating the actual contract with Fischer is unclear, but between 1924 and 1926 the following works by Sibelius were published by that firm: *Five Romantic Pieces* (opus 101), *Five Characteristic Impressions* (opus 103), and *Danses Champêtre* (opus 105).[9] Quite possibly the first visit Nekton had with Sibelius at Ainola was in the summer of 1923, when he and his wife were invited there.

Einari Marvia's careful reading of the Suomi Lodge No. 1 records reveals that the raising of a candidate in three degrees within a single ceremony was not that unusual, especially if the lodge had need of someone's talents. This happened with the initiation of the organist Arvi Karvonen. In September 1922, a special meeting was called, "to which only three Masons took part, including Nekton," so that Karvonen could be raised to the third degree. The reason for this hastily arranged affair was that the lodge had an immediate need of a second organist.[10]

In addition to Linko and Karvonen, the lodge also called upon Wettenhovi-Aspa, Toivo Kontio, and Sibelius to serve as organists on a temporary basis. On those occasions when Sibelius was the organist, much of the music he played was improvised. The Masons in attendance found his improvisations appropriate and inspiring, but they also found them to be too long. Consequently, the Grand Master sometimes had to approach Sibelius at the harmonium and ask him to stop playing so that the proscribed rituals could continue.[11]

Lodge records indicate the names of persons participating in meetings and therefore it is possible to verify when Sibelius attended and when he assumed the duties of organist. For example, he was the organist on 1 November 1922

9    In a letter to Sibelius (5 Dec 1922, in Helsinki University Library Coll. 206.26), Toivo Nekton discusses his contact with Carl Fischer on behalf of the composer. An excerpt from this letter can be found in Dahlström, *Jean Sibelius*. See also Einari Marvia, "Sibeliuksen Rituallimusikki" (1994):228n64. In a letter to Sibelius (17 July 1950) concerning payment of American royalties, Nekton refers again to the Carl Fischer publications: "...you permitted me to bring about your first realization of American royalties in the modest sum of $1500 from Carl Fischer as an advance on the sale of your finest 15 'short' instrumental compositions." This letter is in the "Sibelius Family Collection 36/94," National Archives of Finland.

10   Marvia, *Sibeliuksen Rituaalimusiikki*, 84.

11   Ibid.

when the architect Frans Ilander and the opera singer Johannes Theslöf were initiated in the first degree. He also played on 17 January 1923 when another architect, Eliel Saarinen, was raised in the first two degrees. Both Saarinen and Theslöf were close friends of Sibelius.

Suomi Lodge No. 1 was fortunate to have as members three opera singers—Wäinö Sola, Severus Konkola, and Sulo Raikkonen—who could perform the solo vocal parts of the Masonic music. Wäinö Sola was not among the initial group of twenty-seven who became members of the fraternity in August 1922. His passage through the first three degrees occurred on three separate occasions, with the third coming on the evening of 15 June 1923, when Sibelius was organist. It was then that Sola and others in attendance that evening, such as Toivo Nekton and guests from GLNY, experienced the memorable improvisations for which Sibelius was becoming known.[12]

The wealth of artistic talent represented among the membership of this lodge brought the brotherhood into close contact with many different types of cultural experiences. Whenever an artist exhibited his works or a musician had a concert, it was not uncommon to see the Masons attending those events *en masse*. Such was the case when Sibelius's Sixth Symphony was premiered in 1923. This show of support was not unique among Masons in Finland. It merely reflected a longstanding tradition with the Craft. No clearer example can be cited than the patronage for Mozart's concerts in Vienna, which were heavily subscribed by the Masonic brotherhood of that city.

On his return to Finland in May of 1923, Nekton found that Suomi Lodge No. 1 had leased the upper two floors of a three-story building located at 13 Union Street (Unioninkatu) in Central Helsinki and transformed them into an elegant and functional lodge facility. He also found that those parts of the rites and rituals that he had translated from English into Finnish were now being translated into Swedish. This project was undertaken by a committee of Masons to insure that all future lodge work could be conducted in either Swedish or Finnish, the two official languages of Finland. Eventually five lodges were established in Finland and each chose the language or languages it would use on a regular basis for its work: two chose Finnish, two chose Swedish, and one chose to use both Finnish and Swedish.

In March 1924, the officers of the lodge in Helsinki and the two newly constituted lodges in Tampere and Turku drafted a petition to GLNY for

---

12   Ibid., 20.

a Grand Charter that would allow these three lodges to be constituted as a Grand Lodge. It was an important and necessary step if all the rites of the American system were to be fully executed without involving the authority of an extraterritorial Grand Lodge. Once again the Masons of Finland were indebted to Toivo Nekton, for he willingly added a strong recommendation to the petition before it was submitted to GLNY for consideration. A warrant to establish "an independent sovereign Grand Lodge for Finland" was granted and on 9 September 1924 a delegation from GLNY arrived in Helsinki to mark this historic event. They brought with them a beautifully hand-engraved Grand Charter, the "first and only *grand birth certificate* issued under the Athol Charter held by the New York Grand Lodge."[13] Music for this important and impressive ceremony was provided by Jean Sibelius (organist), Wäinö Sola (tenor soloist), and a group of choral singers.

Sibelius was named Grand Organist of the new Grand Lodge of Finland, but his composing and conducting schedule left him little time to participate in Masonic activities. During his first year of membership, he made an effort to attend a half dozen or more meetings. After that, his participation was often limited to a single meeting per year. Between 1920 and 1926, Sibelius brought forth the last of his major works: Symphonies no. 6 and no. 7, the incidental music to *The Tempest,* and *Tapiola.* During this same period he traveled to London, Rome, Gothenburg, and Stockholm to conduct performances of his symphonic works. With such frenetic activity, it is understandable why Sibelius did not get around to composing music for the Masonic ritual of his lodge.

In the fall of 1926, when Wäinö Sola was with his fellow Masons at a lodge dinner, he suggested to the brotherhood that Sibelius be invited to compose music specifically for their Masonic rituals. His suggestion met with immediate approval and he was authorized to present the proposal to Sibelius. Apparently Sola and other members of the lodge either did not remember or did not know that this request for ritual music had already been communicated to the composer in August of 1922. That notwithstanding, Sola went to Ainola under the impression that he was the first to initiate this idea of having music composed, instead of improvised, by Sibelius. The composer willingly consented to the idea but several more months passed before there was any

---

13   Nekton, "Highlights," 28. See also "The Grand Lodge of Finland," *Masonic Outlook* (March 1925):138, for the Memorial Address, Inaugural Address, and Proclamation read on this occasion.

indication that he was actually working on the score. In an effort to move the project forward, Berndt Forsblom donated 10,000 FM to the lodge for the purpose of commissioning Sibelius to compose the ritual music. Sibelius was paid the 10,000 FM shortly before the end of 1926 and by January of 1927 he had completed the first version of his "Musique réligieuse" that became opus 113.[14]

How long Sibelius worked on preparing the eight pieces that comprise the 1927 ritual music is not known. He was, after all, quite familiar with the rituals and may have simply committed to paper some of the ideas earlier expressed in his improvisations. Marvia believes Sibelius must have worked closely with Sola, Samuli Sario, and other members of the lodge, and that he must have read the marginal notations concerning music that Nekton made in his Finnish translation of the GLNY rituals. If he did neither, it is difficult to explain how Sibelius could have achieved such a perfect interrelationship between music and ritual action, one of the crowning achievements of opus 113. In Marvia's opinion, "mere inspiration would not be sufficient to produce the kind of precision that is required by the ceremony."[15]

There is little information to indicate the sequence in which Sibelius composed the eight sections of "Musique réligieuse." Surviving correspondence confirms that Berndt Forsblom sent Sibelius the poem "On kaunis maa" by Augustus Simelius (Aukusti Simojoki), suggesting it be set to music.[16] Perhaps Forsblom was already familiar with Jaakko Tuuri's 1924 setting of this same text as a duet (opus 8, no. 2) and that may have prompted him to recommend it. Sibelius completed his setting of "On kaunis maa" in December 1926, the earliest date mentioned for any of the sections of opus 113.

---

14  Marvia, *Sibeliuksen Rituaalimusiikki*, 21. Sibelius wrote réligieuse, instead of religieuse, when entering this opus in some of his work lists and therefore the incorrect spelling has been retained in this text whenever the 1927 edition of opus 113 is cited. "Musique réligieuse" was not used as a title for the American editions of 1936 and 1950.

15  [Marvia], "The Ritual Music of Sibelius" [typescript], 2. Sibelius may have been influenced by the corpus of instrumental and vocal music for Masonic use composed and published by Johann Gottlieb Naumann (1741–1801), a Kapellmeister for the Dresden court who also briefly served the courts in Stockholm and Copenhagen.

16  Berndt Forsblom's heirs have two letters that confirm the poem was received by Sibelius and set to music no later than Christmas Eve, 1926. One is from Sibelius, who thanks Forsblom for the poem; the other is from Wäinö Sola, who tells Forsblom the poem he sent Sibelius has been given a lovely setting. Portions of these letters are quoted in Marvia, *Sibeliuksen Rituaalimusiikki*, 200.

It is entirely possible that the remaining seven sections of "Musique réligieuse" could have been composed between the writing of "On kaunis maa" and the first performance for lodge members in January 1927. Any skepticism about how quickly Sibelius could create a composition with such ritual significance as opus 113 may have been laid to rest by his wife in an interview conducted by Anni Voipio in 1940. Aino Sibelius told the reporter that her husband did not make rough drafts of his compositions nor did he work out the thematic materials at the piano. His compositions were simply transmitted to paper after having been fully formed as a complete entity in his mind.[17]

At a Suomi Suur-Loosi meeting on 7 January 1927, Samuli Sario was inducted as Grand Master and it was on this occasion that Sibelius introduced the members in attendance to three pieces from his "Musique réligieuse": the opening hymn "On kaunis maa," the closing hymn "Suloinen aate," and the funeral march "Surumarssi." In Sola's account of this event, he and Ernst Linko were asked by Sibelius to be at the lodge that evening to give a first reading without any prior rehearsal. Sibelius merely gave some suggestions about tempo and then trusted Sola and the organist to perform to his expectations.[18]

Arvi Karvonen also remembered this initial reading of the ritual music, but believed it was he and not Linko who accompanied Sola that evening. Karvonen recalled that he, Sola, and Sibelius met together at the lodge in the afternoon of that same day to decide on suitable registrations for the harmonium.[19] At a point in the score where Sibelius indicates the music should be played triple *forte*, Karvonen did his best to increase the dynamics with the rather limited resources at his disposal. Sibelius, however, thought more sound could be wrung from the harmonium and he began pulling out whatever knobs on the console he could reach. When the full potential of the harmonium had been exhausted and the dynamic level still fell far short of what was desired, the composer

---

17   For Aino Sibelius's remarks, see Voipio, "Sibelius as His Wife Sees Him," *The New York Times* (28 Jan 1940):II, 8, portions of which are quoted on page 16 of the first edition of this book.

18   Marvia, *Sibeliuksen Rituaalimusiikki*, 22.

19   A harmonium is a reed organ activated by air pressure from foot and knee-operated bellows. The size of the reed organ for which Alexandre François Debain patented the name "harmonium" in 1842 was relatively small. Later in the century when builders such as Paul Schiedmayer of Germany constructed two-manual reed organs that were large enough for use in churches and concert halls, the name "harmonium" continued to be applied to this type of instrument. S. v. "harmonium" in *The New Grove Dictionary of Musical Instruments* (1984), II, 131 and III, 221.

vented his displeasure on the instrument.[20] As early as 1923 Karvonen had been instructed to replace the Mannborg harmonium with an organ, but the financial circumstances of SSL did not permit such a lavish purchase until the late 1940s.[21]

Two of the pieces included in opus 113 involved Swedish texts by the poet Viktor Rydberg. After Sibelius set these texts to music, he asked Samuli Sario to translate the Swedish lyrics into Finnish so that his entire composition could be sung in one language. A notation on the score indicates Sario completed his translations on 10 January, just two days before the performance was to take place. On the night of 12 January 1927, members of SSL heard Wäinö Sola and Arvi Karvonen perform for the first time the eight pieces that comprised the original version of "Musique réligieuse." The first and last pieces were solos for the organist. The lyrics for the other six pieces were printed separately in small booklets and given to SSL members so they could fully appreciate what was being sung. Since Sibelius did not place the vocal and keyboard parts together, the musicians had to perform from separate scores.[22] On this special occasion, the Grand Master gave a speech, praising the composer for his many talents and thanking him for the privilege of using the music at the Grand Lodge and at the other lodges under its jurisdiction. He then named Sibelius the first honorary member of SSL.

In the months that followed, Sola created handwritten scores of Sibelius's music for those authorized to use them. The availability of scores meant that Finland's lodges could adopt the "Musique réligieuse" as a regular part of their rituals. Sola and Karvonen became the principal interpreters of opus 113, even performing the music outside the walls of Masonic lodges. For example, during the 1928–29 concert season, Sola included the six vocal sections of opus 113 as part of his recital program presented in a concert hall for the general public. He was accompanied by Karvonen at the harmonium for the Sibelius work and by Pirkko Sola at the piano for the other works.[23]

From 1927 to the present, Masonic lodges in Finland have continued to use Sibelius's music, adding where necessary other musical pieces for those parts of the ritual not originally covered by what Sibelius had composed. By no means,

---

20   Marvia, *Sibeliuksen Rituaalimusiikki*, 22.
21   In addition to the Mannborg harmonium, the lodge also had a Steinway piano that was donated by Berndt Forsblom in 1927. See Marvia, *Sibeliuksen Rituaalimusiikki*, 22.
22   The original 1927 manuscript of opus 113 is in the archives of SSL.
23   Fabian Dahlström graciously supplied a copy of this program.

however, do Finnish lodges feel bound to use opus 113 on a regular basis. A great variety of music is represented in their rituals, much of it composed by other fellow Masons.

Between 1922 when Suomi Lodge No. 1 was constituted and 1927 when Suomi Suur-Loosi was provided ritual music by Sibelius, the lodges in Finland endeavored to follow as faithfully as possible Toivo Nekton's guidelines for the implementation of the American Masonic system for the Craft. These guidelines were primarily in the form of marginal notes and rubric-style addenda to Nekton's Finnish translation of the ritual texts. Of particular interest are those relating to music. He not only indicated where music was both necessary and desirable, but he also suggested how the music might be performed. His directives are often quite precise and no doubt reflect the musical tradition of either the Grand Lodge in New York or the Morton Lodge No. 63 in Hempstead, Long Island (NY), where Nekton held membership. They also reflect his knowledge of the 1904 *Monitor of the Work ... in the Jurisdiction of the Grand Lodge of New York* and the writings about degree work by Denslow, among others. He balanced his keen insight into ritual use of music with his knowledge of the aesthetic tastes of the Masons in his homeland. As a result, the Masonic lodges of Finland were able to incorporate their preference for music performed by a vocal soloist rather than a quartet and to limit choral participation to several well-known Lutheran chorales, which to the present day can form a regular part of their ritual music.

Little reliable information has come to light about the music used at Suomi Lodge No. 1 and Suomi Suur-Loosi prior to the introduction of opus 113. Marvia interviewed persons who had been connected with the Helsinki lodges in the 1920s and he came away with a meager but interesting bit of information. Wäinö Sola and Arvi Karvonen recalled that Mozart's music provided a well-spring for suitable selections, especially those that originally had some connection with Freemasonry. Other composers whose music served as a vehicle for expressing the Masonic lyrics to which they were wed included J. S. Bach, Handel, and Beethoven. Music notebooks in the SSL archives provide evidence that music was also drawn from well-known chorales and hymns.

What role musicians who were members of the lodge had in creating ritual music, either through improvising or composing, is not readily discernible. In the obituary that Sola wrote for his fellow Mason, Ernst Linko, he mentions that Linko set his own music aside as soon as Sibelius's "Musique réligieuse" was completed.[24] If Linko had composed music for lodge work, as Sola implies, no doubt other musicians had also taken their turn at doing the same. Certainly this would have been in the tradition of "speculative" Freemasonry since its beginnings in the eighteenth century.

---

24  Sola's remarks in *Koilliskula* 2 (1968) are quoted in Marvia, *Sibeliuksen Rituaalimusiikki*, 199.

# CHAPTER TWO

# THE BEGINNINGS OF FREEMASONRY IN ENGLAND, AUSTRIA, FINLAND, AND AMERICA

### The Grand Lodge of England

Freemasonry, in its present-day form, had its beginnings in England during the reign of King George I. Members of the Four Old Lodges in London called a meeting in February 1717 for the purpose of appointing one of their number as Grand Master. This event initiated the founding of the Grand Lodge of England on 24 June 1717, the Feast of St. John the Baptist, and eventually the Grand Lodge concept for organizing Freemasonry spread throughout the rest of the world.

Initially the Grand Lodge of England had no permanent place in London for its meetings and therefore it resorted to using inns, taverns, and even one of the city's livery company halls for its Masonic gatherings. Vocal music was an integral part of these gatherings. One of the earliest known Masonic songs, the "Entered Apprentice's Song" ("Come, let us prepare"), appears first under the title "Freemasons' Health" in a collection of songs called *The Bottle Companion* (now in the British Museum). It then appears in what is believed to be its earliest printed version dating from December 1722. The song's melody is patterned after an Irish air and over the years has had different harmonizations, with one by Samuel Holden, published in 1797, being especially favored.[1]

Official songs of Masonry were included in books devoted to rules and rituals. For example, *Anderson's Book of Constitutions*, first published in 1723, has "The Master's Song," along with several other songs, including the "Entered Apprentice Song" mentioned above. Sometimes the music was printed together with the verses for the songs; at other times the verses were printed with only the name of the tune indicated. These early examples were but a prelude to the more than 200 Masonic songs that would be printed in England throughout the eighteenth century, and many of these same songs continued to be reprinted over and over, eventually finding their way into twentieth-century song books.

By 1768 the Grand Lodge of London decided to locate its activities at a permanent site in the city and to that end it formalized plans to erect a building. Funds had to be raised for this project. That is when the Grand Lodge initiated the practice of recording the names of its members and charging membership dues. Ever since, Masons around the world have been charged fees for membership, degree work, and related lodge activities.

Five years passed before land was purchased for the Grand Lodge on Great Queen Street and another three before the building was ready for occupancy. On 23 May 1776 a crowd of Masons and their wives converged on Great Queen Street. The day had finally arrived when they could participate in the dedication of the Freemasons' Hall.[2]

The ceremony was conducted according to traditional Masonic rites and accompanied by appropriate music. Surviving records indicate that a considerable number of musicians participated in the ceremony under the direction of a lodge member, the well-known virtuoso violinist and composer, John Abraham Fisher (1744–1806). Some thirty instrumentalists and an equal number of vocalists, including "five boys from St. Paul's" positioned themselves at one end of the hall and performed a half dozen or more pieces: an instrumental "grand piece" for the formal processions, several choral items, including Handel's coronation anthem "Zadok the Priest" and Fisher's "Grand Anthem." The last named item was based on a paraphrase of Psalm 133, which

---

1    Hamill, "Vocal Music in Craft Ceremonies and After Proceedings," *Ars Quatuor Coronatoram* 88 (1976):188–89.

2    Haunch, "The Dedication of Freemasons' Hall 23 May 1776," *Ars Quatuor Coronatorum* 88 (1976):179.

opens with the words "Behold how good and joyful a thing it is, brethren, to dwell together in unity."[3]

When two of the singers decided to offer their services *gratis* for the ceremony, they were initiated, "by dispensation from the Grand Master," into the first two degrees of Masonry several days prior to the dedication ceremony. A candidate's benefit to a lodge often took precedence over the standard rules for attaining membership and therefore it was not unusual to have candidates raised in the first three degrees in this manner.[4]

Use of the Freemasons' Hall was not confined to Masonic activities. For over one hundred years, the Hall was the scene of balls, banquets, meetings, and most notably a series of subscription concerts known as the "Freemasons' Concerts." From the very beginning of modern or "speculative" Freemasonry, music played an important and prominent role, and it has continued to play that role wherever Masons assemble for their rites and rituals.[5]

A comparison of ceremonies conducted in eighteenth-century lodges with those conducted in Finland two centuries later reveals striking similarities in the way musical material was positioned to support and complement the ritual action. Here, for example, is a description of how the Lodge of Antiquity conducted a ceremony in Mitre Tavern on 5 March 1777:

> Lodge opened in the Third Degree in an adjacent Room, a Procession entered the Lodge Room, and the usual ceremonies being observed, the Three Rulers were seated. A piece of music was then performed, and the 12 Assistants entered in procession and after repairing to their stations the Chapter was opened in solemn form. Brother Barker then rehearsed the Second Section. A piece of music was then performed by the instruments. Brother Preston then rehearsed the third section. An Ode on Masonry was then sung by three voices. Brother Hill rehearsed the fourth Section, after which a piece of solemn music was performed. Bro. Brearly rehearsed the fifth Section, and the funeral procession was formed during which a solemn dirge was played and this ceremony concluded with a Grand Chorus. Bro. Berkley rehearsed the sixth Section, after which an anthem was sung. Bro.

---

3   Ibid., 180.
4   A similar situation occurred when Jean Sibelius and Ernst Linko were initiated into the Craft.
5   Haunch, 181.

Preston then rehearsed the seventh Section, after which a song in honour of Masonry, accompanied by the instruments, was sung. The Chapter was then closed with the usual solemnity, and the Rulers and twelve Assistants made the procession round the Lodge, and then withdrew to an adjacent Room, where the Master's Lodge was closed in due form.[6]

William Preston, a name well known to historians of Freemasonry, presided over this ceremony, which included at least eight musical numbers. Some were for instruments alone; others were for voices with instrumental accompaniment. One, performed by "three voices," may have been an *a cappella* number; another was a choral number. "Funeral music" was also included because this ceremony involved raising one or more candidates for the Third Degree.

In the latter part of the eighteenth century, William Preston, William Hutchinson, and Wellins Calcott expressed concern over the lack of regularity and refinement in the wording of Masonic rituals conducted by lodges in England. To remedy this situation, each man set himself the task of publishing what he considered to be an improvement upon current practice. Calcott was the first of the three to publish his work. His *Candid Disquisition* appeared in 1769 and the wording of some of the rituals found therein are very similar to those still in use today. Calcott's book was also reissued in Boston in 1772 to over 400 subscribers and thus it became an important source for lodge work on both sides of the Atlantic.[7]

## Freemasonry in Austria

The spread of Freemasonry in Europe was surprisingly rapid. Not even the Church of Rome's condemnation of the Craft in the Papal Bull of 1738 could slow its progress. Nowhere was this progress more pronounced than in France and in the Habsburg controlled lands of Austria, Bohemia, and Hungary. These were the very countries against which the Bull had been directed. Coincidentally, these same countries saw fit to suppress the promulgation of

---

6   This quotation, from a Prestonian Lecture delivered by Ivor Grantham in 1950, appears in Sharp, "Masonic Songs and Song Books of the Late XVIII Century," *Ars Quatuor Coronatorum* (1952):90.

7   McLeod, "Wellins Calcott, and His List of the Officers of Lodges and Provincial Grand Lodges, 1772," *Transactions: American Lodge of Research* 16 (1986):86.

the Papal Bull as soon as it was issued, thereby making it possible for Catholics to actively embrace Freemasonry.

The first lodge in Austria was founded in 1742 and for the next fifty years Freemasonry blossomed and flourished in that part of Europe. One of the staunchest defenders of Freemasonry in Austria was Francis Stephen, Duke of Lorraine, who had become a member of the Craft in 1731. Although the Duke's wife, Empress Maria Theresa, and his son, Joseph II, disapproved of Freemasonry, they nevertheless tolerated its presence on Austrian soil throughout their lifetimes.[8]

The first significant move against the Austrian lodges came in March of 1781. Joseph II issued an imperial decree that forbid "secular and spiritual orders" to be under the jurisdiction of, or to engage in any financial transactions with, a foreign authority. This decree had the effect of forcing the Austrian lodges to sever their ties with the Grand Lodge in England, under whose influence they had been organized and whose rituals they had adopted. In compliance with the decree, the Grand Lodge of Austria was constituted 22 April 1784.

A second and more troubling order was handed down by Joseph II in December of 1785. By this time there were eight "St. John" lodges in Vienna, with a membership drawn from some of the most highly respected and influential persons in that city.[9] Wolfgang Amadeus Mozart was associated with two of them: the "Zur Wohltätigkeit" ("Charity"), where he was initiated in the First Degree, and "Zur wahren Eintracht" ("True Concord"), where he was passed to the Fellow Craft Degree on 7 January 1785.[10] The Emperor thought the Masons, by their very presence, were becoming too powerful in Vienna. Consequently, he moved to curtail what he perceived to be a threat from the eight "St. John" lodges, which at the time had a combined enrollment of a thousand members. The Emperor ordered the number of lodges in all cities under his rule be limited to three and he further limited the number of members each could enroll. By the beginning of 1786, the eight lodges had realigned themselves and reduced their membership to less than four hundred. In the process, the lodges also eliminated many positions of authority within

---

8   Chailley, *The Magic Flute, Masonic Opera*, 60.
9   Membership lists survive. See Landon, *Mozart and the Masons*, 5, 8, and 25.
10  Franz Joseph Haydn was invited to become a member of the "Zur wahren Eintracht" lodge.

the Masonic hierarchy, which is exactly what the Emperor most wanted to achieve.

Mozart wrote a number of works in which he incorporated Masonic ideas and symbols. The most famous of these, *Die Zauberflöte* (*The Magic Flute*), he composed in 1791. This opera was designed both to entertain and to enlighten the Viennese aristocracy about the workings of the Craft. Other works were composed to entertain the brotherhood on occasions of special celebration. In this category are the following Masonic compositions which Mozart entered in his thematic catalogue for the year 1785: "Die Maurerfreude" (KV. 471), a cantata for tenor, male chorus, and orchestra, first performed at the "Zur gekrönten Hoffnung" ("Crowned Hope") lodge in honor of Ignaz von Born; "Lied zur Gesellenreise" (KV. 468) for voice and organ, written in honor of Leopold Mozart one month before he was to be passed in the Second Degree at a lodge in Vienna; and the incomplete cantata "Die Seele des Weltalle" (KV. 429/468a) for tenor, male chorus, and orchestra. Another cantata, *Laut verkünde unser Freude* (known as *The Little Masonic Cantata*, KV. 623) that represents the last completed work entered in Mozart's catalogue, was performed in November 1791 on the occasion of the consecration of the temple for the "Zur neugekrönten Hoffnung" ("Newly Crowned Hope") lodge. Mozart conducted this performance just two days before his death.[11]

Although Mozart did write several compositions that were, or could have been, used within the context of a Masonic ritual, he never produced an entire opus to accommodate the eight or more places in regular lodge work where music is a necessary component. This may come as a surprise to Masons who throughout this century have used *Mozarts Kompositionen für Freimaurer* in which selected segments of Mozart's music have been adapted for all aspects of their lodge work.[12] Even during Mozart's lifetime, Masons in Vienna had started adapting his non-Masonic music for their use, simply by adding suitable Masonic lyrics. Examples include his "De profundis clamavi" (KV. 93), "Ave verum corpus" (KV. 618), and "O heiliges Band" ("Lobegesang auf die feierliche Johannisloge," KV. 148/125h). So effectively was this done that over time Masons looked upon the adaptations as music originally created by Mozart for the Craft.

---

11    Landon, 56.
12    See Reinecke, ed., *Mozarts Kompositionen für Freimaurer*.

Several works by Mozart may have been written to serve a ritual function. They include two songs for male chorus, "Zerfliesset heut' geliebte Brüder" (KV. 483) and "Ihr unsre neuen Leiter" (KV. 484). These were composed in December 1785 as opening and closing "odes" marking, respectively, the opening of the new "Zur neugekronten Hoffnung" lodge and the closing of his own "Zur Wohltätigkeit" lodge, as required by the Emperor's reorganization plan. Mozart's "Lied zum Gesellenreise" (KV. 468), although written to be sung when his father was passed to the Fellow Craft Degree in April 1785, could have been used ritually to welcome Second Degree candidates at subsequent degree-raising ceremonies.

Mozart's *Maurerische Trauermusik* (KV.477/479a) should also be considered in the category of ritual music. At one time this *Masonic Funeral Music* was thought to have been composed to honor the memory of two famous Masons—Franz, Count Esterházy of Galántha, and George August, Duke of Mecklenburg—who died within a day of each other in the latter part of 1785. Reportedly the first performance of this orchestral score took place on 17 November 1785 at the "Hoffnung" lodge where a "Lodge of Sorrows" was convened.[13] Since this event took place several months after his *Trauermusik* was composed (ca. July 1785), it is obvious that Mozart originally intended it for something other than the deceased Masons' memorial service.

In his recent study of eighteenth-century Viennese lodges, Heinz Schuler concludes that no separate occasion was set aside to commemorate the death of a fellow Mason. That being the case, he further concludes that Mozart's *Trauermusik* must have been specifically composed for ritual work related to the third degree. The date given this work in Mozart's catalogue is 12 August 1785, a date that also coincides with the raising of some Masons to the Master's level in a ceremony held at the "Zur Wohltätigkeit" lodge.[14]

Mozart's Masonic opera was a huge success in Vienna, but it did little to forestall Masonry's inevitable fate within the Habsburg realm. The sudden death of Leopold II in 1792 spawned rumors that the Freemasons had poisoned him. Leopold's successor to the throne needed nothing more than rumors to justify abolishing Freemasonry. In 1795 the Court Chancellor ordered all Masonic lodges closed and they remained closed until 1918.

---

13  Landon, 18–20.
14  See Schuler, "Mozarts Maverische Trauermusick KV 477/479a: Eine Dokumentation," 46–70.

## Freemasonry in Sweden and Finland

When a former Grand Master in England, the Duke of Wharton, immigrated to France in the 1720s, he brought with him the rituals and constitution of the Grand Lodge of England. These Masonic documents were translated from English into French and formed the basis upon which newly created lodges in France were organized. Although the earliest French lodges adhered to the English rituals, they nevertheless were considered to be "irregular" lodges because they worked without warrants from the Grand Lodge of England. Not until 1732 was a warrant granted for a "regular" lodge in France.

Foreign visitors to France during the late 1720s and 1730s were curious about Freemasonry and eager to learn what they could about the Craft, often accepting invitations to become initiates. Among those who investigated and ultimately embraced Masonry while in residence in Paris were several Swedish noblemen. Upon their return to Sweden, Count Axel Wrede-Sparre and Count Knut Posse brought with them the French translation of the English rituals. This became the basis for the Swedish Rite which developed into a similar but unique form of Craft Masonry. From the founding of the first "irregular" Masonic lodge in Stockholm in 1735 to the present, Freemasonry has been allowed to exist in Sweden without interruption.[15]

Within the next twenty-five years several more lodges were constituted in Sweden, including the first "regular" lodge in 1752 and the St. Augustin Lodge in 1756. Although the last named lodge was founded in Stockholm, it was actually intended for the city of Turku (Åbo) in Finland. The lodge began its work on Finnish soil in 1758 and by the end of the eighteenth century additional lodges had been founded in Helsinki. At just the time Freemasonry was gaining a foothold in Finland, war broke out between Sweden and Russia. Although the war was of short duration (1808–1809), its consequences were disastrous for the Finnish people who, for over 400 years, had been culturally and politically linked with Sweden. By the terms of the peace treaty, Russia was allowed to annex Finland.[16]

Many who held membership in the Finnish lodges were officers of the Swedish army stationed in Helsinki and Turku. When the war with Russia ended in 1809, these officers were recalled to Sweden, and this resulted in a

---

15   Ekman, *Highlights of Masonic Life in Nordic Countries*, 27–33.
16   Klinge, *A Brief History of Finland*, 50–57.

mass exodus of Masons from Finland. Their departure, however, did not cause the demise of the Finnish lodges. It was a decree from the Russian Czar that inflicted the fatal blow.

When Czar Alexander created the Grand Duchy of Finland, he let the Finnish people believe that their homeland was an autonomous entity wherein existing laws and customs would continue to be honored. There were, however, some important exceptions. Not the least of them was that Freemasonry would no longer be tolerated. At first, the Czar's ban extended only to Masonry on Finnish soil, but by 1822 the Czar had banned the Craft from the entire Russian Empire. That ban lasted one hundred years. Freemasonry was not reintroduced in Finland until 1922.[17]

### Freemasonry in America

Masons in England lost little time in bringing the Craft to the American colonies. As early as 1730 the Duke of Norfolk appointed the American-born Daniel Coxe to be Provincial Grand Master for the region covered by three colonies—New Jersey, New York, and Pennsylvania. Among others who were to hold this position was Benjamin Franklin.[18]

New York had to wait for more than fifty years before it had its own Grand Lodge. Although a Provincial Grand Lodge was established there in 1781, it took another six years before that same Masonic organization could declare itself free and independent of the Grand Lodge in England. The outcome of the Revolutionary War had not only championed the cause of liberty; it also helped the cause of Freemasonry as well.

Many of the more important Masonic books originally published in England were reissued in the American colonies. One was Wellins Calcott's *A Candid Disquisition*, cited above. Another was Benjamin Franklin's edition of *Anderson's Constitutions*, first printed in England in 1723. Others included works by William Preston, along with various "monitors."[19] These publications

---

17   Ekman, 48–51. For an informative article that touches on the attitude of Freemasons in Russia toward the forces that shaped "man's moral nature," see Garrad, "Karamzin, Mme De Stael, and the Russian Romantics."

18   See Lipson, "The Americanization of Freemasonry."

19   See Calcott, *A Candid Disquisition*; Anderson, *The Constitutions of the Free-Masons*; and Preston, *Illustrations of Masonry*.

served to guide the workings of American lodges, but they did little to prevent lodges from creating their own versions of the rituals.

By the beginning of the nineteenth century, the lack of uniformity in the rituals for New York State lodges had become of particular concern to the Grand Master of the GLNY, DeWitt Clinton, who was then Governor of New York State. To remedy this situation, Governor Clinton appointed a committee to visit the lodges within his jurisdiction and to instruct the members therein how to properly execute the rituals. Unfortunately the committee could not agree upon which version of the rituals to promote and thus the project was abandoned. Individual Masons, however, did try to systematize the workings of the lodges. Thomas Smith Webb's *The Freemason's Monitor* and Salem Town's *A System of Speculative Masonry* are two such publications. Along with these books came also Masonic song books such as David Vinton's *Masonick Minstrel* and Luke Eastman's *Masonick Melodies*. The end result was that Americans were able to fashion their own rituals for the Craft, making them similar to, but distinct from, those in England.

Masonry flourished after the colonies declared their independence from England, and the growth in the founding of new lodges continued until the "William Morgan Affair" of 1826. Thereafter, a period of anti-Masonic activity ensued, forcing the closing of many lodges, especially in New York State.[20] Those members who remained active embarked on an ambitious campaign to rid themselves of derogatory images, not the least of them being that of the "merry Mason." Following the Civil War, Masonry once again gained its respectability and by the turn of the century there was a huge increase in membership.

This increase, however. had more negative than positive aspects to it. There were so many men who were eligible to pass through the various degrees that Masonry became essentially one ritualistic activity after another, leaving little time for fellowship and the building of communal relationships. By the 1920s, American Freemasonry came to a crossroads. Some of the membership wanted to retain the fraternity as a strictly moral and religious institution. Others wanted to transform the fraternity into more of a civic-minded institution that "would dedicate itself to service beyond the walls of its temples."[21] This debate over the future course of Masonry came at a time when huge sums of money

---

20  Carnes, *Secret Ritual and Manhood in Victorian America*, 22–25.
21  Dumenil, *Freemasonry and American Culture 1880–1930*, 170.

were being spent on erecting both magnificent Masonic temples for lodge meetings and extensive buildings to care for orphans and widows. For the next several decades, Masonry was able to maintain a balancing act between the inward and outward manifestations of the Craft.

The lodge buildings in use during the first half of the twentieth century varied considerably in size, design, and elegance. Some were small, simple, clapboard buildings constructed in the eighteenth century.[22] Others were large modern buildings. For example, the facility housing the Grand Lodge of New York epitomizes the grandeur of the environment in which Masonic rituals could be conducted in this period. Its Grand Hall, one of the best acoustically-designed auditoriums in New York City, was equipped with an Austin pipe organ in the balcony that made it possible to perform festive music for ceremonial events. Individual lodge rooms within the Grand Lodge facility were also elegantly designed, each with its own pipe organ.[23]

It was the custom in New York to have the ritual music performed not just by a "Grand Soloist" and a "Grand Organist" but by a combination of various musical forces: the organ alone; a male quartet (TTBB) whose members often took solo parts, and the assembled group of Masons with the organ either doubling or accompanying the vocal parts. For special occasions such as the annual Grand Lodge ceremonies, well-known male quartets from other New York lodges would be invited to perform. Also invited were male choruses such as the Schenectady Masonic Chorus, which frequently traveled to New York to provide entertainment for social events organized by the lodge.[24]

Reports of these annual events seldom indicate what music was performed for the rituals. Even less information exists concerning the music chosen for the degree rituals that took place on a regular basis throughout the year. Masonic monitors and song books were in rich supply throughout the nineteenth and twentieth centuries and from them it is possible to reconstruct the sights and sounds of lodge meetings, Masonic social gatherings, and Masonic funeral ceremonies. The music performed came primarily from four sources: church hymnody, folk songs, musical excerpts by classical composers, and newly

---

22   An example of this type of construction can be seen in the lodge built in 1797 at Bridgewater, NY.

23   When the cost of keeping all of these pipe organs in good repair rose to prohibitive levels, the smaller pipe organs in the individual lodge rooms were replaced by some very modest electronic instruments. Only the Austin pipe organ in the Grand Hall has been retained.

24   "Music at Grand Lodge," *Masonic Outlook* (June-July 1937):198.

composed works by Masons. As mentioned above, most Masonic song books were arranged according to lodge functions, so even the least skilled musicians had little difficulty in selecting appropriate music.

In the Robert R. Livingston Masonic Library (formerly known as the Grand Lodge Library and Museum) can be found additional sources from which the ritual music was drawn. One was the previously cited *Mozarts Kompositionen für Freimaurer*. This 73-page collection, edited by Carl Reinecke and published in Germany at the beginning of the twentieth century, contained four excerpts from *Die Zauberflöte* together with other Masonic pieces by Mozart, including those discussed above. Among the multiple copies of this edition in the LML is one with the name of Marshall Kernochan stamped on the cover. Inside his copy there is a separate sheet of music paper on which Kernochan has written how the Mozart music was to be coordinated with the work of the Craft. He even indicated what measures should be used as an introduction for each piece and what voices should sing the music. In addition to the nine selections taken from the Reinecke edition, Kernochan indicated that eleven pages from the piano-vocal score of *Die Zauberflöte* were also to be used. The final item in his list is not by Mozart; it is "Now sing we," a song that appears in many well-known Masonic collections.

With its lyrics in German, the Reinecke edition, by itself, could not have been the source from which the lodge singers performed. Extant materials at LML suggest that the singers relied upon handwritten copies of music prepared by Bruno Huhn. These copies contained the requisite vocal parts from both Reinecke's *Kompositionen* and Mozart's *Die Zauberflöte*. In place of the German lyrics, Kernochan supplied English lyrics. The keyboard accompaniment was not written out; it was simply cued in the vocal parts. Since Huhn's adaptation for male voices adhered closely to the original scores, the accompanist could play his part directly from the printed music.

Also preserved in the LML are new works composed by several Masons who were associated with the Grand Lodge in New York City. In addition to those by Kernochan, a substantial number were composed by Bruno Huhn (1871–1950), an ASCAP composer and organist.[25] Huhn frequently took well-known Masonic texts and set them to music, creating an interesting corpus

---

25   Bruno Huhn was a pianist and conductor of several choral groups in the New York City area. He also composed songs, choral works, anthems, piano, and organ music. See *ASCAP Biographical Dictionary*, 4th ed. (1980):240.

of materials for ritual use. Many of Huhn's Masonic works cite Kernochan as
the creator of the lyrics. These handwritten scores exist in multiple copies and
probably were sung at the GLNY by the Bruno Huhn Quartet.[26] Although
this cache of musical materials is relatively small, it clearly demonstrates that
the musical activity occurring in connection with the rituals may have been of
a much higher quality than the contents of various Masonic song books known
to have been available at the GLNY prior to the start of World War II seem
to suggest.

---

26  In 1933, Charles Johnson (Grand Secretary) initiated what became known as "the
    phonograph project" to make available suitable recordings for small lodges. Four such
    recordings were made under the direction of Marshall Kernochan "who not only organized
    the quartet, selected the music, but also paid the bill of $600." S. v. "Sibelius" file at LML:
    letter from Charles Johnson to S. Nelson Sawyer (14 Feb 1934).

# CHAPTER THREE

## THE 1936 EDITION OF
## *MASONIC RITUAL MUSIC*

In the 1920s and 1930s when Masons from the GLNY made their official visits to SSL, they had the possibility of becoming acquainted with Sibelius's "Musique réligieuse." They may even have had the good fortune to hear this music sung by Wäinö Sola and accompanied by Sibelius at the harmonium. Charles Johnson, Grand Secretary for the Grand Lodge of New York, visited Finland in 1933 and heard a well-known organist play Sibelius's music composed for the three degrees in the lodge room in Helsinki. This experience made such a memorable impression on him that he was moved to introduce this musical gem into the ritual at the GLNY.[1] On his return to New York, Johnson wrote a letter to SSL's Grand Secretary, Toivo Kontio, to thank him for his hospitality. In that letter of 22 March 1933, Johnson also asked if a copy of Sibelius's music could be made available for ritual use at the GLNY.[2]

Kontio never had an opportunity to respond to Johnson's request because he died soon after receiving the Grand Secretary's letter. Johnson waited patiently

---

1    In a report submitted for publication in the *Proceedings of the Grand Lodge* (May 1935):38, Charles Johnson invokes the editorial "we" to disguise the fact that it was primarily his initiative that brought the gift of Sibelius's score to the GLNY. S. Nelson Sawyer, who also heard Sibelius's music when he was at the Helsinki lodge in 1933, wrote to Johnson (13 Feb 1934) and suggested copies of "Musique réligieuse" be procured for use at GLNY. Sawyer cautioned that if copies were obtained, GLNY would be expected to copyright the music in order "to protect it from general publication." In Johnson's reply (14 Feb 1934) to Sawyer, he reveals that contact with SSL had been made a year ago to no avail and therefore he was sending another letter that very day with the same request. S. v. "Sibelius" file at LML.
2    Letter from Charles Johnson to Toivo Kontio (22 March 1933) in SSL archives.

for his request to be acted upon by Kontio's successor, Arvo A. Aalto, but after almost a full year had passed and no response was forthcoming from SSL, Johnson wrote again to Aalto and restated his request for a copy of Sibelius's music.[3] Another year passed without any acknowledgment of this second letter. Finally, on 6 March 1935, Johnson received a letter from Aalto, which contained the news that he had waited so long to hear.

Aalto begins his letter with an explanation of why a year had lapsed between the receipt of Johnson's letter and his response. He attributes the delay to the particular terms under which Sibelius's ritual music could be performed. According to Aalto, when Sibelius completed "Musique réligieuse" in January 1927, he "dedicated" the eight compositions "to the Suomi Lodge ... with the reservation that they were not to be used anywhere else." For this reason, Aalto could not respond to Johnson's request until he had obtained the composer's consent to extend the privilege of ritual use of "Musique réligieuse" beyond the confines of SSL. Aalto further explains that "a suitable time or occasion for making the request to our famous composer had not appeared before recently."[4] After mentioning that a complete score was on its way to New York, Aalto expresses his pleasure on behalf of SSL "to send something of our own," as a way of acknowledging indebtedness to the Grand Lodge for past favours: "This music is one of our biggest assests [sic], which we are happy and proud to own."[5]

Aalto's use of the word "own" has been interpreted by some members of SSL, among others, to mean copyright ownership. This interpretation unfortunately has been so ingrained in the minds of some Masons in Finland that it is difficult to convince them of what Sibelius intended, namely that the eight compositions that comprise the totality of the 1927 version of opus 113 were "dedicated" to, and "reserved" solely for the use of, the lodge in Helsinki. "Dedication" does not mean copyright ownership, nor does "reserved use" imply a copyright restriction.

A handwritten copy of "Musique réligieuse" was sent to the GLNY in a package addressed to Axel Solitander, Grand Master of SSL, who planned to be in New York City in late March. The idea was to have Solitander personally

3    Letter from Charles Johnson to Arvo A. Aalto (14 Feb 1934) in SSL archives.
4    Letter from Arvo A. Aalto to Charles Johnson (6 March 1935) in LML. In the SSL archives are Wäinö Sola's letter to Axel Solitander (27 Feb 1935) and his note to Sibelius (28 Feb 1935), both of which concerned Johnson's request for a copy of the ritual music.
5    For excerpts form Aalto's letter, see Appendix I.

present the Sibelius score to the Grand Master of the GLNY on behalf of the Masons of Helsinki. Aalto indicates that a "covering letter" would also be sent with the manuscript. What that letter contained is not known, for the letter does not seem to have been preserved in either the GLNY or SSL archives.

On 7 April 1935, Solitander was in New York City to make the official presentation of a bound manuscript copy of Sibelius's opus 113 to the GLNY.[6] On the outer title page are the words "Masonic Ritual Music," followed by "composed for the Grand Lodge of Finland by R∴W∴ Bro. Jean Sibelius." Directly beneath these words is "respectfully Jean Sibelius," written in the composer's hand. The inner title page has "Masonic Ritual Music composed by R∴W∴ Bro.," written in Sola's hand, but beneath those words is "Jean Sibelius," in the hand of the composer. Neither title page includes the opus number or the word "copyright."[7] According to Aalto's letter, "the final shape of the gift" was the responsibility of "our Grand Singer, Wäinö Sola." By this he meant that the copy was prepared by Sola, a fact that Sola himself acknowledges in an article written as a memorial tribute to Sibelius:

> In 1935, with Sibelius' permission, I was entrusted with the task of making a complete copy of the music which was then sent in an artistic edition, bound in leather, as a token of gratitude to the Grand Lodge of New York which had reintroduced the idea of freemasonry in Finland.[8]

---

6   Axel Solitander provides a description of the day's events in his letter to Wäinö Sola (7 April 1935) in the SSL archives. At least one other manuscript copy representing the original version of Sibelius's Masonic music was given as a gift to a Masonic organization in America from the Masons in Finland. According to a letter (11 Dec 1946) of thanks to Sibelius from the president of The Philalethes Society in Los Angeles (CA), the Master of St. Henrick Lodge No. 5 in Helsinki had presented a bound volume of Sibelius's ritual music, autographed by the composer, to this exclusive international society of leading Masonic writers and editors. In appreciation for the manuscript, Sibelius was elected the first honorary member of The Philalethes Society. S. v. letter from W. A. Quincke, together with Sibelius's membership card and note of thanks, in "Sibelius Family Collection 36/94" National Archives of Finland.

7   This manuscript will hereafter be referred to as MS-113-35. See Appendix II for a description and number assigned to each of the manuscripts, photostats, and editions of opus 113.

8   Sola, "Jean Sibelius as a Composer of Freemason Music," 44–45.

Since the ritual used by SSL and the other lodges in Finland was based on a translation of the authorized Masonic text used by the GLNY, the New York Masons were not expected to have any difficulty adapting Sibelius's score to their rites. Nevertheless, Sola offered to come to New York to teach the Masons how to perform the music and where to position the individual pieces. Aalto also included with his letter a guide to the ritual use of opus 113. This guide is of particular value for it suggests how Sibelius's music might have been incorporated into the rites in SSL.[9]

In the absence of the covering letter which supposedly accompanied the Sibelius manuscript, Aalto's letter of March 6th takes on added significance. It clarifies the following points: (1) Sibelius dedicated his opus 113 score to SSL; (2) he was directly involved in the decision to send this music to the GLNY; (3) he alone was responsible for lifting the restriction placed on the ritual use of his music; and (4) he authorized Wäinö Sola to prepare the presentation copy of his vocal-organ/piano score. Last, but not least, the willingness of Sibelius, Sola, and other members of SSL to allow the Masons in New York to incorporate "Musique réligieuse" into their ritual implies tacit recognition that additional copies would have to be made.

The manuscript sent to GLNY has the same eight compositions that comprised the initial verison of Sibelius's opus 113, as presented to SSL in January 1927. It also includes the chorale "Den höga himlen," which probably was composed as early as 11 June 1927.[10] Sibelius was among a group of composers asked to contribute to a revised edition of chorales set to Finnish and Swedish texts. He chose to set Jacob Tegengren's "Den höga himlen," which is simply a Swedish translation of Simo Korpela's "Suur' olet, Herra," first published in 1904. Unlike the other sections of opus 113 that are either for organ alone or for solo voice with organ accompaniment, this added composition is a four-part chorale scored for an *a cappella* (SATB or TTBB) chorus. In other words, Sibelius retains the vocal format required for the book of chorales published in Helsinki in 1927.

---

9    This brief one-page guide for ritual use of the music is preserved in LML.
10   There is an entry in Sibelius's diary on 11 June 1927 indicating the completion of a chorale. Fabian Dahlström communicated to the author that he believes the entry refers to "Den höga himlen." See also Dahlström, *Jean Sibelius.*

It is believed that "Den höga himlen" was first performed for the general public at a festival concert on 9 June 1929. [11] In that same year, this four-part chorale appeared in print in a collection of chorales edited by John Sundberg and published in Helsinki for use in the Evangelical-Lutheran churches. Over the course of the next few years, "Den höga himlen" became a regular part of the ritual music used by SSL and because of this it was included as part of MS-113-35, albeit in Swedish and in the four-part (*a cappella*) chorale form. [12]

Einari Marvia, who spent many years of research on opus 113, claims that certain restrictions were attached to the giving of the 1935 manuscript. Marvia does not question Sibelius's desire to send his manuscript to New York. What he does question is the procedure followed by the GLNY in receiving the gift. According to Marvia, when Solitander presented the manuscript, he "pointed out that the only condition attached to the gift, which had been raised by the composer, was that the music would not be published without his permission." Marvia believed that Solitander had asked the GLNY to confirm this verbal agreement by signing a written consent and sending it to Sibleus. [13] A brief note to Johnson, written by Solitander from his hotel in Washington, D.C., shortly before he was to return to Finland, seems to lend credence to Marvia's interpretation of this situation. The note opens with these words:

> This is intended to serve as a little reminder of the kind promise you gave about a letter regarding Sibelius' music. I would appreciate it very much having to give Br. Sibelius some kind of a report on my arrival to Finland. [14]

Given the close bond that had always existed between the GLNY and SSL, it is difficult to imagine that the officers of the GLNY would ever

---

11   Ibid. For a discussion of a version of this chorale by Sibelius for male quartet and organ accompaniment that was completed circa October 1944 and for another version created by Marshall Kernochan in 1950, see Williams, *Sibelius and His Masonic Music* (1998):197–98.

12   It should be noted that when the original eight pieces of opus 113 did not fully satisfy the needs of the Masonic ritual, Sibelius found it necessary to add more music, such as this chorale.

13   In his letter to the GLNY (11 Feb 1973), Marvia quoted excerpts from Solitander's written summary of the presentation event in New York and then asked if the GLNY had any record of the "consent" form, because none was known to exist at SSL. A copy of Marvia's letter is at LML.

14   Letter from Axel Solitander to Charles Johnson (12 April 1935) in the "Sibelius" file at LML.

have entertained the idea of publishing the "Masonic Ritual Music" without Sibelius's permission, especially when the person who would have been charged with that responsibility was a Mason deeply committed to the musical life of the Grand Lodge. That person was Marshall Kernochan (1880–1955), then vice-president and later president and owner of Galaxy Music Corporation.

Whether or not Solitander delivered to Sibelius a verbal agreement, as Marvia claims, is impossible to prove. If he did and if such an agreement were intended to be fulfilled by a written consent form, then that part of the legal process seems not to have taken place. No written agreement specifically acknowledging a publishing ban has been found in the files of the GLNY or SSL. What has been preserved is the letter Charles Johnson wrote to Solitander and SSL on behalf of the GLNY to express appreciation and thanks for Sibelius's music. A portion of that letter reads:

> If it is satisfactory to you and Brother Sibleius, it would be our thought to print the music privately.... We will undertake to have this edition protected by copyright for the United States.[15]

By asking Sibelius and SSL to find his proposal satisfactory, Johnson offers them an opportunity to voice their objections before he proceeds with the publication. He may have worded his proposal in this way to avoid the kind of delay that accompanied his request for a copy of Sibelius's music in the first place. He had no intention of waiting another two years for a reply to this query. Silence would mean consent. Johnson also acted on his promise to protect the rights of the composer. A certificate of copyright was filed on 3 June 1935. Under "owner of the American copyright" for "Masonic Ritual Music" is written "Free, Ancient, and Accepted Masons, Grand Lodge of the State of New York."[16]

---

15  This excerpt is quoted in a letter from Einari Marvia to the GLNY (11 Feb 1973) in LML. Marvia also quotes what is supposed to be the first part of this same excerpt in his "Ritual Music of Sibelius," but the words appear as follows: "Unless you or Brother Sibelius have any objections, we have thought to publish the music privately for the sole use of the lodges." Since Johnson's letter of 9 April 1935 to Axel Solitander would most likely have been written in English, it is peculiar that Marvia gives two different versions of the excerpt quoted above. Interestingly, Johnson's letter cited by Marvia is reportedly missing from the SSL archives, along with some other documents that Marvia used for his research.

16  A copy of the certificate of copyright for the 1935 manuscript, filed by Galaxy on behalf of the GLNY, is in LML. See also *Catalogue of Copyright Entries*, New Series, vol. 30, no.

If Sibelius's music were to serve the purpose for which it was freely given, then multiple copies were needed so it could be performed by the GLNY as well as by other lodges in the United States. As Johnson's letter indicates, the GLNY lost no time in deciding that a printed edition would offer the most expedient means of reproduction. This, of course, was in sharp contrast to the means used in Finland from 1927 to 1962. Whenever copies of opus 113 were needed for lodges in Finland, they were created by hand, most often by the hand of Wäinö Sola.

Before the 1935 manuscript was placed in a vault at the GLNY to protect and preserve it in as pristine a condition as possible, Marshall Kernochan had a photostat copy made of it. On the cover of this photostat he has written:

> Correct Copy: The original presentation copy of this work, from the Grand Lodge of Finland, contains a very large number of errors and omissions. No performance should be given without comparing the sheets used with this copy, in which all corrections are indicated in red, above the staves.[17]

To signal those corrections, Kernochan placed an asterisk above the staff where each had been made. A majority of the corrections involved the addition of accidentals.

On 25 April 1935, at a "Stated Communication" of the American Lodge of Research in New York, Marshall Kernochan reported that the first presentation in America of Sibelius's "very simple but great 'Masonic Ritual Music' would occur at the Autumn meeting." He further explained that the manuscript would "be published for the benefit of the Craft if there be no infringements on copyright permits."[18] What was not mentioned in the printed version of

---

7, 1935: Part 3—Musical Compositions, p. 732. Receipts confirming the filing were sent to the GLNY with a cover letter (1 August 1935) from Marshall Kernochan. Prior to the expiration of the copyright in 1964, Clarence Laubscher of Galaxy Music Corp. wrote to the GLNY requesting the 1935 copyright registration card so that, if desired, he could file for a renewal. The card was sent on 17 August 1962. See letters dated 22 June, 13 and 17 August 1962 in the "Sibelius" file at LML. Instead of the GLNY filing the renewal, Sibelius's wife and children filed the renewal on 22 May 1963 under renewal No. R315916, with an expiration date of 2010.

17   This photostat copy will hereafter be referred to as C–113–35.
18   "Stated Communication for 29 April 1935," *Transactions: The American Lodge of Research* 11(Feb 1934–Sept 1935):21.

Kernochan's report for this date was the private performance of the "Masonic Ritual Music" on this same evening before a select group of members of the American Lodge of Research. Presumably the words were sung in Finnish, for it was some time after this date that the score was fitted with English lyrics. The only record of this April performance is a description of the event given in the letter which the GLNY wrote to Sibelius on 18 May 1935.[19]

The manuscript (MS-113-35) presented to the GLNY was essentially a copy of the ritual music then in use at SSL. It therefore came with all of the lyrics in Finnish and, in the two sections that set the poems of Victor Rydberg, the lyrics were also given in Swedish, the native language of this poet. Before Sibelius's music could serve any useful purpose for members of the GLNY, the Finnish texts had to be translated into English. Marshall Kernochan asked his friend George (Yrjö) Sjöblom to prepare a translation from which new lyrics could be created.[20] According to Marvia, Sjöblom did more than make a literal translation of the Finnish texts. His English texts were readily adaptable to the musical material and therefore Kernochan had only to make minor revisions in order to create suitable lyrics.[21] For this reason, Marvia believed the published edition should have given some credit to Sjöblom for his work.[22] This, however, did not happen; the edition credits Kernochan as the sole author of the English lyrics.[23]

---

19    Marvia refers to this letter correctly on page 63 of his *Sibeliuksen Rituaalimusiikki*. When he cites the letter on page 211 (in the list of archival holdings of SSL), he mistakenly indicates it was written by Solitander.

20    Letters from Marshall Kernochan to George Sjöblom (21 Sept 1955) and from George Sjöblom to Wäinö Sola (8 Oct 1935) concern the translation of the Finnish texts. A portion of the second letter is quoted in Marvia, *Sibeliuksen Rituaalimusiikki*, 64. Both letters are in the SSL archives. See also a letter from Sjöblom to Arvo Jacobson (3 Oct 1948), in which a request for another translation of these same texts is discussed. This letter is in Appendix I.

21    From extant papers in the "Sibelius" file at "'LML, it appears that Kernochan typed out the Finnish lyrics for each of the six vocal pieces in a manner that showed the proper underlaying of the original text. He left ample space above each line of the Finnish lyrics so that an English translation could be inserted. This meant Sjöblom was able to create a suitable translation without having to consult the vocal lines of the score. For a letter explaining why Sjöblom, who was not a Mason, provided the translations, see chapter eight.

22    [Marvia], "The Ritual Music of Sibelius," [typescript], 12.

23    In a brief article that Kernochan wrote for *Masonic Outlook* (May 1937):178, he assumed full credit for the lyrics, stating that "the English texts have been carefully paraphrased by the writer from the original Finnish."

For the most part, Sjöblom and Kernochan were able to fashion lyrics that fit well with the rhythmic and melodic contour of Sibelius's melodies. Whenever the lyrics did not fit the melody, the music instead of the text was changed. For example, if the English lyrics contained fewer syllables than the Finnish, Kernochan reduced the number of notes in the vocal part to accommodate those lyrics. This type of reduction occurs in the second measure of "On kaunis maa" ("How fair are Earth") where a quarter note has been substituted for two eight notes in the original score and a half note for two quarter notes.

Before the edition was actually in print, members of the American Lodge of Research were treated to a concert version of the "Masonic Ritual Music," performed on 30 September 1935 in the Grand Hall of the GLNY. The August-September (1935) issue of *Masonic Outlook* announced this event, from which the following excerpt is taken:

> This will be a noteworthy occasion, for it will be the very first time, before any American audience, that this music has been heard, and the Craft in this Jurisdiction will have this rare privilege through the courtesy of M∴W∴ Axel Solitander, Grand Master of Finland, cooperating with M∴W∴ Charles H. Johnson. R∴W∴ Marshall Kernochan, Steward of the American Lodge of Research, has in hand the preparation of the Sibelius presentation, including the translation of the words, arranging for the organist and quartette, and superintending rehearsals.[24]

On the occasion of this premiere performance, lodge members expressed their deep appreciation for the gift that Sibelius had given them by making the composer a Fellow of the American Lodge of Research.[25]

This token of esteem was not the only attention that Sibelius was receiving from Americans in the year in which he was to celebrate his seventieth birthday. On 24 November 1935 the results of a nationwide poll among listeners of the Sunday afternoon broadcasts of New York's Philharmonic-Symphony Society concerts were published in *The New York Times*. Listeners were asked to rank their favorites among the symphonic composers featured on the WABC radio broadcasts. The results from the more than 12,000 respondents in the two-

---

24  "American Lodge of Research," *Masonic Outlook* (Aug-Sept 1935):12.
25  "Stated Communication for 30 September 1935," *Transactions: The American Lodge of Research* 11 (Feb 1935–Sept 1935):23.

week poll showed Sibelius topped the list of composers, followed by Beethoven and Ravel.[26]

To mark Sibelius's seventieth birthday, the Philharmonic-Symphony Society of New York broadcast a program on 8 December 1935 that included the music of the top three favorite composers in the audience poll. Sibelius was represented by his Second Symphony (D major), which the orchestra performed under the baton of Otto Klemperer. This nationwide broadcast from Carnegie Hall was also heard in Finland.

The Sunday edition of *The New York Times* for 8 December 1935 noted the composer's birthday with two articles about him. One entitled "Sibelius at Seventy" was written by the music critic Olin Downes. His remarks focused on both the renewed vitality that Sibelius had brought to the symphony and the intra-personal communion the composer had with nature.[27] The other article appeared in the magazine section of the *Times*. The author, Harry Rogers Pratt, praised Sibelius for bringing Finland to the attention of the whole world and considered the composer to have acted as an unofficial ambassador of Finland. Pratt interviewed Sibelius in Finland for this article and by so doing was able to convey to the reader a feeling for the environment in which the composer worked. For example, he described how Sibelius did most of his composing in a study that was located directly over the living room in his home. In response to Pratt asking if he would care to send a message to his friends and admirers in America, Sibelius indicated he would, for he was especially pleased that Americans had shown so much interest in his music. If his compositions could, in some small way, bring the people of America and Finland closer together, then that would be reason enough for him to find happiness on his birthday.[28]

The following day *The New York Times* carried two more articles about Sibelius. From Berlin came the news that Adolf Hitler had awarded the Goethe Medal for Science and Art to the composer, with the actual presentation of the award taking place in Finland.[29] It seems a bit ironic that Germany waited until 1935 to honor the artistry of one whose music had all but vanished from the concert programs in that country. Not only in Germany but also in other

---

26  "Behind the Scenes," *The New York Times* (24 Nov 1935):IX, 25.

27  Downes, "Sibelius at Seventy," *The New York Times* (8 Dec 1935):22.

28  See Pratt, "Hardy Finland Speaks Through Sibelius," *The New York Times Magazine* (8 Dec 1935):16, as well as page 48 of the first edition of this book where Sibelius's remarks are quoted.

29  "Hitler Awards Medal to Composer," *The New York Times* (9 Dec 1935):26.

countries on the continent, Sibelius's style of composition had fallen out of favor by the 1930s. Despite this, Germany's premier music publisher, Breitkopf & Härtel continued to reap huge profits from the sale of the composer's works, most especially from *Valse triste*.

From Helsinki (Helsingfors) came the report of the nation-wide festival that was held in honor of the composer's birthday and broadcast from Finland to America.[30] Over 8000 people had crowded into an auditorium to pay tribute to Sibelius and to hear a concert of his music performed by two orchestras and a chorus of 500 singers. On this occasion Sibelius was the recipient of the highest honor that his homeland could bestow—a laurel wreath given by the Premier of Finland. He also received expressions of appreciation and admiration from colleagues in America. This included the special anniversary issue of *Uusi Suomi* prepared by George Sjöblom, which contained letters of tribute from, among others, Leopold Stokowski, Walter Damrosch, Olin Downes, Nicolai Sokoloff, Richard Aldrich, A. Walter Kramer, and Marshall Kernochan.[31]

In the editing of Sibelius's music for use by the GLNY, Kernochan did more than correct the errors in the manuscript copy and revise the melodic material to accommodate the English lyrics. He created choral arrangements (TTBB) for two of the nine compositions, "Onward, ye Brethren!" and the chorale "The lofty Heav'n." Both arrangements required a change of key to accommodate the vocal range of tenor and bass parts. The reason why Kernochan felt the need to make these arrangements is that music for Masonic rituals at the GLNY was usually sung by a male quartet, in unison or in four parts, rather than by a solo voice. Marvia contends there is nothing to indicate that Sibelius would have approved of these choral arrangements, and indeed no correspondence or other documentation has come to light to contradict that observation.[32] Nevertheless, it seems highly improbable that Kernochan would have considered adding his arrangements to a score by a world famous composer without asking permission, especially when that score was being prepared for publication.

Charles Johnson became ill in 1936 and was confined to a hospital for a considerable period of time. During this confinement, he received two letters from Arvo Aalto, neither of which is preserved at LML, although a copy of the

30  "Finland Observes Sibelius's Birthday," *The New York Times* (9 Dec 1935):26.

31  By special arrangement with *Uusi Suomi*, these same tributes from "leaders in American music" were published simultaneously in English in "Homage to a Master," *Musical America* (10 Dec 1935):5–6.

32  [Marvia], "The Ritual Music of Sibelius," [typescript], 12.

one dated 29 September 1936 is in the SSL archives. Since Johnson was too ill to write to Aalto, he had his secretary, Mathilde Fisher, respond on his behalf. In her letter of 9 October, Fisher first explains why Aalto has not heard from Johnson and then she writes the following:

> In regard to our acknowledgment to Mr Sibelius, Mr. Johnson will take this matter up when he leaves the hospital and endeavor to raise some money. The purpose for which it is to be used will be left entirely to you.[33]

In the absence of one of Aalto's letters to Johnson, Fisher's words will have to remain somewhat of a mystery. Marvia believes the "endeavor to raise some money" was being undertaken to satisfy a royalty agreement between the GLNY and Sibelius. If one looks at the next sentence, a different interpretation can be offered, namely, that the raising of money may have been intended as a charitable donation for a cause to be determined at a later date by SSL. Nothing in Fisher's words suggests that the money pertains to royalty payments, and since the edition was not yet in press, any question concerning "profits" would have been a bit premature.

The exact date of publication for *Masonic Ritual Music* is not known, but it is generally assumed the score appeared sometime between December 1936 and May 1937. The edition could not have appeared before 2 December 1936, for that is the date when a certificate of copyright was recorded for the printed edition.[34] This new copyright was claimed "on the additional numbers and additional revisions." In other words, the 1936 copyright protects Kernochan's contribution to the edition: the correction of errors in the manuscript Sibelius sent to the Grand Lodge; the addition of English lyrics; the revision of the vocal parts to fit the new lyrics; and the addition of the two TTBB choral arrangements of nos. 6 and 8.

Galaxy printed the music for the 1936 edition but contracted with Gettinger Printing to make the covers. Gettinger's bill for printing 1030 covers is dated 29 May 1937.[35] Although this bill may have been issued a considerable time

---

33   Letter from Mathilde Fisher to Arvo A. Aalto (9 Oct 1936) in SSL.
34   See *Catalogue of Copyright Entries,* New Series, vol. 31, no. 12, 1936: Part 3—Music Compositions, p. 1440. The cover of the first edition of *Masonic Ritual Music* carries two copyright dates: 1935; rev. ed. 1936.
35   S. v. "Sibelius" file at LML.

after the Galaxy order was filled, it nevertheless raises the possibility that copies of the score were not available from the publisher before this date.

The preface to the 1936 edition makes clear that GLNY would restrict the distribution of copies: "In making this royal gift, the Grand Lodge of Finland requested that the music be used solely for Masonic purposes and we shall use every endeavor to see that it reaches only duly accredited Masons who, we feel sure, will be only too glad to keep faith in this respect."[36] To insure that only "duly accredited Brethren" were allowed to purchase the edition, Masons had to obtain their copies directly from the office of the Grand Secretary.[37]

On 3 June 1937, after the first edition of *Masonic Ritual Music* was published, Charles Johnson wrote a letter to Axel Solitander with information that subsequently initiated considerable debate over its meaning. The portion in question reads:

> The Sibelius music which we received at your hands was found to be most beautiful. We have had it copyrighted so that no one could copy it and have had it prepared for use in the Lodges. A brother has paid for this work and all profits which may come from its sale will be sent to you, either for the Grand Lodge or to Brother Sibelius, as you may see it. I am sending you some copies so that you may see how it has been prepared.[38]

Marvia uses the letter quoted above to fault the Masons in New York for waiting so long to inform SSL about the 1936 edition, for he assumed, incorrectly, that the copyright and publication dates of the GLNY edition were one and the same. He writes: "… only later in the following year, on 3 June 1937, was Solitander informed of the publication, and the information was relayed quite indiscriminately in one sentence amidst the rest of the text."[39] Since the edition may not have gone to press until April or May of 1937, one can hardly fault Johnson for a delay in announcing the publication. Nor can one claim, as Marvia has done, that this information about publication and copyright came as a complete surprise to SSL and Sibelius. Johnson's letter of

---

36   For the complete preface, see Appendix II.
37   Kernochan, "*Masonic Ritual Music* by Sibelius," 178.
38   Letter from Charles Johnson to Axel Solitander (3 June 1937) in the SSL archives. Marvia quoted this excerpt in his letter to the GLNY (11 Feb 1973).
39   [Marvia], "The Ritual Music of Sibelius," 12.

9 April 1935, discussed earlier, clearly stated the Grand Lodge's plans for the English-language edition.

If the GLNY had to rely on the generosity of one of its members in order to print the edition, it seems a bit optimistic of Johnson to expect any profits from the sale of a score that could be used only in Masonic rituals. While it is not known what Johnson intended by his remarks concerning profits, it is well documented that Sibelius did not enter into a formal written contract with Galaxy for printing the first edition of his score. He therefore would not have been in a position to claim or expect a specific percentage of royalties or profits, if any should have materialized.[40]

Although Johnson does not give the name of the brother who "paid for this work," other sources suggest that it was Marshall Kernochan who provided the funding. Many years later, in a letter written to Toivo Nekton on 31 July 1949, Kernochan stated that he had created the English lyrics for the Masonic ritual music and donated them without charge to the Grand Lodge for use in the 1936 edition. He also mentioned that the Lodge paid Galaxy for printing "at cost" copies of this same edition and that a generous contribution was made anonymously to the Grand Lodge with the intention that this would help defray the printing costs.[41]

What profits could have accrued from the sale of the score is impossible to ascertain. Arvo Aalto was very interested in the financial aspects of the edition and in reply to his queries, Johnson freely supplied facts and figures. In correspondence dated 2 May 1938, he stated that $80.75 had been realized from the sale of copies. This rather modest sales figure caused Johnson to add the following comment: "Of course you understand that the fine type of music in this collection is not likely to be popular. We have hopes that there will be enough music lovers among the organization of Masonic lodges to clear up our supply."[42]

---

40    See chapter nine, where a letter from Toivo Nekton to R. Rowlands, dated 7 August 1950, mentions the subject of royalties for Sibelius from the 1936 edition.

41    For this letter, see KFC.

42    Letter from Charles Johnson to Arvo A. Aalto (2 May 1938) in LML. In this same letter Johnson states that "the cost of printing, engraving, etc." was $156.85, but he does not mention the cost of the covers for the edition. The implication of this letter is that the cost of the edition would be deducted from the sales figure before any profits could be discussed or possibly any royalties paid. Johnson was fully aware of the $45 charge for the covers. He mentions it in a note to Marshall Kernochan (1 June 1938), in which he requests "the cost for publishing the Sibelius Ritual Music. The figures are desired so that we may answer an

The market for copies of either the first or the second edition was reasonably small, a fact admitted by Kernochan in his memorandum written in 1949: "Since the Masonic versions are sold exclusively to Masons ... the market is obviously an extremely limited one." [43] Proof of his statement comes from information published in the 1950s showing copies of the first edition were still being sold even after the second edition appeared in print. Not until the early 1970s was the supply of the 1936 edition exhausted. [44]

Johnson's letter of June 1937 quoted above mentions that copies of the score were to be sent to SSL, but those copies apparently never reached their destination. At least that is what is implied in a letter from Aalto to Johnson on 5 April 1938: "As we have not heard anything lately regarding the printed music and the reception it has received, our Grand Master directed me to ask you in this connection to let us have some information about it, which information we would be very anxious to have as well for ourselves as for Bro. Sibelius." [45]

Marvia contends that if the copies had arrived at SSL there would not have been a need for Aalto to request news about the printed edition. To further substantiate his premise, he mentions that Sola knew nothing of the edition and therefore kept making handwritten copies of the score a decade or more after the American edition was printed. He argues that if Sola had known about or had had access to the 1936 edition, he would have had no reason to continue writing out the score to satisfy requests for it from other lodges in Finland. In making his case, Marvia seems to have overlooked a *very* important point. The 1936 edition had English lyrics and a vocal part adapted to those lyrics. Therefore it would have been of little use to those who required the ritual to be sung in either Finnish or Swedish.

Aalto's letter of 5 April 1938 also mentions receipt of a telegram from Olin Downes, in which he requests permission to present at the World's Fair the

---

inquiry from the Grand Secretary of Finland." Galaxy complied with the request by issuing a statement dated 24 June 1938 that detailed the previously quoted amount of $156.85. S. v. "Sibelius" file in LML.

43  See item 7 of Marshall Kernochan, "Memorandum. For reference in case R∴W∴ Jean Sibelius should at any future time desire a written contract with Grand Lodge with reference to this Ritual Music." No date is given, but this memorandum was written prior to January 1950. Relevant sections of this document are quoted in Appendix I.

44  Letter from Wendell K. Walker to Puavo Heikkila (3 June 1974). A copy of the original letter is in LML.

45  Letter from Arvo Aalto to Charles Johnson (5 April 1938) in the SSL archives. A copy was made available to the author.

choral version of "Onward, ye Brethren!" (No. 6a of the *Masonic Ritual Music*).
Downes was chairman of the music division for the New York World's Fair and
he wanted music by Sibelius performed both for the "Preview" event scheduled
on 1 May 1938 and for the official opening of the Fair in 1939. For over thirty
years, Downes had steadfastly promoted Sibelius's music to American audiences
through his position as music critic for *The New York Times*. Now the New York
World's Fair offered him the most prestigious stage of all on which to place his
idol.

# CHAPTER FOUR

## ONWARD, YE PEOPLES!
## THE INFLUENCE OF DOWNES AND SJÖBLOM

Olin Downes first heard the music of Sibelius in 1907, when he was music critic for the *Boston Post*. In that year, he reviewed a program given by the Boston Symphony Orchestra with conductor Karl Muck and it included Sibelius's Symphony no. 1. Downes was immediately captivated by the depth of emotion and breadth of design flowing from this score and it made him eager to hear more compositions by this Nordic symphonist. Little did Downes realize that his enthusiastic response to Sibelius's music in 1907 would become a life-consuming passion for him until the year of his death in 1955.

At the end of 1923, Downes left the *Boston Post* and joined the staff of *The New York Times*, becoming its chief music critic. This new position gave him access to the optimum medium in which to promote Sibelius's music. His knowledge of the composer soon extended far beyond the realm of scores, recordings, and live performances. Through an extensive amount of correspondence, supplemented by an occasional personal visit, Downes was able to develop a very close and enduring friendship with Sibelius and his family.

The initial meeting of Downes with the composer occurred in 1914 at the Norfolk Festival, where Sibelius conducted the premiere of his *Oceanides*. This event led Downes to comment that it was "one of the few occasions when he felt himself in the presence of a genius of world class."[1] This performance of

---

1    Tawaststjerna (Layton, trans.), *Sibelius*, II, 275.

*The Oceanides* convinced Downes that "Sibelius had the power to bring to life the innermost soul of the music."[2]

Subsequent meetings with the composer took place in Finland, with Downes making his first visit to Ainola in September of 1927, a second in 1929, and a third in the summer of 1932. Before returning home after the 1932 visit, Downes wrote a letter to Sibelius asking permission to bring back to America three of the composer's choral works to share with Hugh Ross (1898–1980), the conductor and director of the highly acclaimed Schola Cantorum with which he was associated from 1927 until 1971. Sibelius's choral and vocal compositions were not readily available outside of Finland, primarily because there was little demand for works with Finnish or Swedish lyrics. Downes obviously was interested in promoting the non-symphonic works of Sibelius and hence his request on behalf of Ross.

The amount of effort Downes had been expending to focus attention on the music of Sibelius was gaining recognition on both sides of the Atlantic. On 6 December 1936 the *New York Herald Tribune* carried an article by Lawrence Gilman entitled "Sibelius in America."[3] The article was written to counter claims made repeatedly in the British press that the music of Sibelius would seldom be heard outside of Finland were it not for British conductors and musicians including his works on their programs. Gilman poses the question of whether or not those in Britain know about "a penetrating and courageous music critic" who for years has been telling the American public that Sibelius is a great composer? Gilman continues with his own claim that no one in the English-speaking countries had been more successful than Downes in championing the merits of the Finnish composer.[4]

Beginning in the 1920s, Sibelius and his music had steadily gained in popularity in the United States. The government of Finland was well aware of the role Downes had played in bringing the music of Sibelius into the center of American cultural life. In appreciation for his efforts, Finland honored Downes, granting him in 1937 the title of Commander of the Order of the White Rose.[5]

---

2    Ibid., I, 107.
3    Gilman, "Sibelius in America," *The New York Herald Tribune* (6 December 1936).
4    Ibid.
5    *The New Grove Dictionary of American Music*, s. v. "Downes, (Edwin) Olin."

Credit for the popularity of Finnish music in general and of Sibelius's music in particular in the post World War I era belongs as much to George (Yrjö) Sjöblom as it does to Olin Downes.[6] Surviving correspondence to and from Sjöblom in the 1920s and 1930s makes clear that it was this expatriate who paved the way for Downes to establish a meaningful relationship with Sibelius. George Sjöblom (1889–1971) joined the staff of *The New York Times* as a proofreader in 1926, two years after Downes came to work for that same newspaper. While proofreading may have been his profession, promoting and managing Finnish musicians who wanted to perform in America was Sjöblom's all-consuming avocation and for his untiring efforts in this regard, he was awarded the Order of the White Rose medal by the Finnish government. With his fluency in both the Finnish and English languages, Sjöblom was able to participate fully in negotiating Finnish-American cultural exchanges. This also meant that he and Sibelius could communicate directly whenever the need arose, whereas Downes always had to work through an interpreter.

It was in his role as secretary for the Humanitas Society for Art and Literature (formerly the Sibelius Club) that Sjöblom found himself involved with events relating to the composer's career.[7] In 1925 a member of the Humanitas Society, Henry Holm of Hancock, Michigan, spearheaded a plan to bring Sibelius to America to conduct his compositions. The first target of this plan was the Philadelphia Orchestra, whose members were to form an ensemble for the sesquicentennial celebrations planned for the city in the summer of 1926. The initial contact with the orchestra produced a favorable response, which was then followed up with additional communications from Henry Holm in February of 1926, all of which was shared with Sjöblom as secretary of the Society.[8] Encouraged by this first step in implementing his plan, Holm asked Sjöblom to contact the manager of the Philharmonic-Symphony Society of New York to find out if an American tour for Sibelius could be arranged.

Before engaging the manager of New York's Philharmonic-Symphony Society in a discussion about the proposed American tour, Sjöblom decided to find out if anyone else might be planning a similar project. What better person

---

6   For more about Sjöblom's role in promoting Finnish music in America, see Williams, "George (Yrjö) Sjöblom: Jean Sibelius's Link with America."

7   Letters and papers relating to the Sibelius Club and the Humanitas Society for Art and Literature are privately held by the Sjöblom family in the Sjöblom Family Collection (SFC).

8   Letters in SFC.

to ask than Downes, who would surely know, or could find out, the answer to this question. Although Sjöblom and Downes worked for the same newspaper, they apparently did not make a practice of discussing matters relating to Finland at the office. Instead, they kept their relationship on a somewhat formal basis, preferring to communicate with each other by letter or in carefully scheduled meetings. Downes replied to Sjöblom's query in a letter dated 16 April 1926. He indicated his willingness to give him any information he could "relating to a possible American tour next season for Jean Sibelius" and suggested they set up a meeting to discuss the matter.[9] As it turned out, Downes did not have any information to share, which left Sjöblom to pursue the matter on behalf of the Humanitas Society on his own. To that end, he asked Downes for a letter of introduction to George Engles, manager of the Philharmonic-Symphony Society of New York. Downes gladly complied and his letter dated 22 April 1926 introduces Sjöblom "as a member of the Finnish Humanitas Society for Finnish Art and Literature who is interested in arranging a tour next Fall in America for Jean Sibelius."[10] Engles met with Sjöblom and, although he did not react adversely to the idea of a tour, eventually had to conclude that the proposal did not warrant encouragement. In his letter to Sjöblom of 10 May 1926, he wrote: "I do not believe there would be sufficient financial return to warrant making an offer to Mr. Sibelius for a tour as guest conductor in this country."[11]

Throughout this period of negotiations, it is doubtful that Sibelius expressed the same degree of enthusiasm about an American tour as did his friends and promoters. Some hint of this comes when Downes writes to Sjöblom on 2 July 1926 and asks: "Have you heard anything from Jean Sibelius's state of mind as regards an American concert tour next winter?"[12]

The somewhat restrained tone of the correspondence between Sjöblom and Downes that survives from the first half of 1926 belies the friendship that was developing between them. Although Downes was three years older than Sjöblom, he always seemed to go out of his way to express his gratitude for the kindnesses shown him by the Sjöblom family. Examples of this are found in his letter of thanks for two gifts (a book, *Finland and Its People*, and a picture of

9   Letter from Olin Downes to George Sjöblom (16 April 1926) in SFC.
10  Letter from Olin Downes to George Engles (22 April 1926) in SFC.
11  Letter from George Engles to George Sjöblom (10 May 1926) in SFC.
12  Letter from Olin Downes to George Sjöblom (2 July 1926) in SFC.

Sibelius) received in July 1926; a postcard sent from Helsinki on the occasion of his first visit to Finland in 1927; and a letter to Tyyne Sjöblom, George's wife, dated 30 December 1930. In his letter to Mrs. Sjöblom, Downes writes: "I am grateful to you for the encouraging letter you have written me about my articles on Sibelius."[13]

George Sjöblom also served as the New York correspondent for *Uusi Suomi* published in Helsinki. In 1935 he prepared a special issue of *Uusi Suomi* to honor Sibelius on the occasion of his 70th birthday. Sjöblom contacted friends and associates of the composer to write personal tributes. One of the persons contacted was Marshall Kernochan, who inquired of Sjöblom about the desired length of these tributes. Sjöblom's reply, given in a letter of 4 October 1935, reads:

> I would estimate the maximum space at the disposal of UUSI SUOMI to be about 3,000 words per each contributor. The shortest tribute received to date is from Stokowski, who writes exactly 25 words. Walter Damrosch uses about 75. Others have written longer letters. Mr. Olin Downes, my colleague, is preparing a fairly long article. I would like to leave the matter up to your own judgment—provided you would not exceed 3,000 words.[14]

In the late 1930s several events propelled Sibelius's popularity to new heights. Not the least of these was the 1939 New York World's Fair. Olin Downes was appointed to the chairmanship of the music division for the fair and in this role he helped plan many events, including one promoting the official opening of the fair. It was a gala "Preview" held on Sunday, 1 May 1938. The event began with a gigantic parade that formed at Battery Park and wound its way to the Queensborough Bridge. The fair's colors of orange, blue, and white dominated the scene, as a million people lined the parade route to share in the festivities.[15]

The fair itself was located at Long Island City where buildings representing the "City of Tomorrow" were nearing completion. The fair grounds were opened to the public for this special "Preview" day and two separate musical

---

13   Letters and postcard in SFC.
14   Letter from George Sjöblom to Marshall Kernochan (4 Oct 1935). S. v. "Sibelius" file at the LML.
15   "1,000,000 Watch Preview Parade," *The New York Times* (1 May 1938):I, 35.

programs were scheduled to entertain the visitors. The afternoon pageant, devised by Herbert Graf and directed by Charles Allen, was free and held outdoors on a specially constructed stage. In front of the stage was an oval enclosure with seating for 3,000 people and beyond this enclosure stood an audience estimated to number 10,000. The program began with trumpeters playing the fanfare from Act III of Verdi's *Othello*. This heralded the entrance of folk dancers, marchers representing 54 different nations, bands, and singers drawn from nine different choral groups. After the 400 folk dancers had performed in their colorful costumes and the guest soloists had sung selections from some Broadway shows, a grand finale was staged.[16] It began with the Martha Graham dancers, followed by a high school chorus singing George Gershwin's "The Dawn of a New Day," commissioned as the fair's theme song. Finally the 600-voice chorus, conducted by Hugh Ross, sang (with Sibelius's permission) "Onward, ye Peoples!" This was the first public performance of the work and it served as the composer's formal "salute" to the fair.[17] In the month preceding the Preview concert, Ross had completed an *a cappella* SATB version of "Onward, ye Peoples!" and presumably it was his choral version that was adapted for this special performance.[18]

Later that same evening, the 500 singers of the Schola Cantorum and the Oratorio Society joined forces with New York's Philharmonic-Symphony Society to perform, among other works, Beethoven's Ninth Symphony. Although only two thousand people could be accommodated in the building where the concert was held, the music was heard by many more thousands, made possible by broadcasting the evening's program to the nation. Olin Downes's remarks to the audience that night about the day's purpose were also broadcast.[19]

On 2 May 1938 *The New York Times* carried on its front page an article about the previous day's music festival. Included in the article was a statement about the use of music to promote one of the themes of the fair, namely that

---

16   "500,000 Visit Fair at Music Festival," *The New York Times* (2 May 1938):1, 19.

17   For a description of this event, see "World's Fair Festival Today," *The New York Times* (1 May 1938):X, 5. Not mentioned in the newspaper accounts was the presence of a concert band that provided the accompaniment for this mixed chorus arrangement of "Onward, ye Peoples!"

18   Galaxy Music Corp. filed a certificate of copyright for a single copy of Hugh Ross's unpublished choral arrangement on 11 April 1938. See *Catalogue of Copyright Entries* 33 (1938):549 (no. 12836). Apparently this arrangement was never published.

19   "500,000 Visit Fair at Music Festival," *The New York Times* (2 May 1938):19.

of peace and good-will as interpreted by the great masters of that art. Other articles in this same newspaper revealed that messages of peace and good-will were not being heard in Europe. May Day was celebrated in Germany in a far different manner than at the World's Fair. Hitler used the occasion to boast of his power. The Nazis were on the move and before the end of the decade all of Europe and Scandinavia would be confronted with the threat of war.[20]

In the same week that Sibelius was honored at the World's Fair Preview, he was also honored by the Masons in New York City. The annual awarding of the Grand Master's Medal and Scroll "for a Masonic Brother who had made an outstanding contribution in the field of fine arts" took place at the Grand Lodge. Previous awards of the Grand Master's Medal (now known as the Grand Lodge Medal for Distinguished Achievement) had gone to a painter, a poet, an engraver, and an author. Only one medal was awarded each year. Sibelius was named the 1938 recipient and news of this event was carried by *The New York Times*.[21]

Among the citations read in Sibelius's honor was one by Marshall Kernochan:

> You have preserved with peculiar power in these modern days of confusion and surrender to things transitory and tawdry, the true spirit of the bards of old who caught the echoes of eternal truth and sent them vibrating through the world on the wings of musical sound.[22]

Another read by the Grand Secretary Edward Carmen contained these excerpts:

> R∴W∴ Jean Sibelius, loyal and distinguished citizen, … confers on you its special Grand Master's medal for outstanding achievement in the art of music.… Master of technique, you have resisted the temptations of mere virtuosity and, listening to the promptings of your own inner nature, have given to the world undying music of

---

20  "Germany Gains Listed by Hitler," *The New York Times* (2 May 1938):3.

21  "Daniel Beard Gets Medal of Masons," *The New York Times* (5 May 1938):24. Of the five who received various medals on this occasion, Sibelius's special honor received very little attention in this article, probably because he was unable to attend.

22  "Sibelius…Composer…Freemason," *Empire State Mason* 5 ("Holiday Issue," 1957):18.

simple dignity, breath, and poetic charm.... we hail you as a man of unswerving integrity, a Brother of patient courage, and a composer of the most inspiring symphonic music of our time.[23]

Since Sibelius could not attend the award ceremony, his medal and scroll were sent to Finland for presentation to him at a special ceremony hosted by SSL in Helsinki. Kernochan arranged to have the Grand Secretary's citation translated into Finnish by George Sjöblom so it could be read in the composer's native language at that event.[24]

Plans to include a choral composition by Sibelius for the fair's festivities began at least as early as March of 1938. On the 22nd of that month Downes sent a telegram to Sibelius, asking for permission to present the No. 6 chorus of the *Masonic Ritual Music* at the New York World's Fair "Preview." He added that his request was supported by "a very great Mason, Marshall Kernochan."[25] Einari Marvia believes that Kernochan, on behalf of Galaxy, may have initiated the permission request because he sensed the commercial potential from such a venture. Apparently Sibelius lost no time in responding to Downes because, on the 30th of March, Downes sent another telegram to Sibelius alluding to the composer's consent.[26]

Shortly after receiving Downes' telegram of March 30th, Sibelius contacted SSL to find out if there were any objections to the performance of the No. 6 hymn for the fair. In a letter dated 4 April 1938, Grand Secretary Arvo Aalto replied to Sibelius's inquiry and admitted he had already communicated the consent of SSL to Downes in a telegram. That telegram (undated) reads:

RETELLS SIBELIUS WE AGREE/STOP/REGARDING FINANCIAL PROCEEDS CONTACT NEW YORK GRAND LODGE GRAND SECRETARY/GRAND LODGE OF FINLAND[27]

---

23  *Proceedings of the Grand Lodge of New York* (1938):136.
24  In a letter to George Sjöblom (29 April 1938), Marshall Kernochan expressed his appreciation for the translation of the citation. This letter and a copy of the Finnish translation are in SFC. Both English and Finnish versions of the citation are also in the "Sibelius" file at LML. See Appendix I.
25  Marvia, *Sibeliuksen Rituaalimusiikki*, 201.
26  Ibid.
27  This telegram is in the SSL archives and a copy was made available to the author. The two telegrams which Downes sent to Finland and the letter from Arvo Aalto to Jean Sibelius (4

Arvo Aalto reaffirmed approval of the performance request in this excerpt from his letter to Charles Johnson of 5 April 1938:

> Bro. Sibelius has kindly consented to this and his as well as our consent has been cabled to Mr. Downes with the request that he may communicate with you regarding the financial proceeds. I have taken the privilege of troubling you with this matter in order that the arrangements may conform with the previous ones agreed upon between you and our M∴W∴ Grand Master.[28]

Marvia and others have pondered what previous arrangements had been agreed upon. Did these arrangements pertain to the publishing of the entire *Masonic Ritual Music* or did they pertain to negotiations between Galaxy and Sibelius for the publishing of one or two items from the *Masonic Ritual Music* for non-Masonic use? It would seem that the latter scenario is closer to the truth.

Based on an interview with Marshall Kernochan for *The New York Times*, Noel Straus reported that Kernochan (president of Galaxy), A. Walter Kramer (managing director of Galaxy), and Charles Johnson had conceived the idea to publish a non-Masonic version of "Onward, ye Brethren!" for mixed chorus long before the music was considered for the Preview concert.[29] Since a choral arrangement (TTBB) of "Onward, ye Brethern!" (No. 6 of the *Masonic Ritual Music*) had already appeared in print, they reasoned correctly that Sibelius would agree to have a non-Masonic version placed under contract with Galaxy, thereby assuring the composer of royalties. To accommodate non-Masonic use of the music, only a few changes had to be made to the lyrics. An example of the kind of changes Kernochan made can be seen in the opening line where "Onward, ye Peoples!" has replaced "Onward, ye Brethren!"

---

April 1938) are also in the SSL archives.

28 Letter from Arvo A. Aalto to Charles Johnson (5 April 1938) is in the "Sibelius" file at LML.

29 Noel Straus, "Sibelius Score," *The New York Times* (3 Oct 1948):II, 7. Copies of the typescript of this article are in the "Sibelius" file at GLNY, which suggests Straus had to gain permission from GLNY before releasing his article for publication. If this were the case, it seems strange that GLNY would have sanctioned an article that contained a number of factual errors.

As early as April 1938, Galaxy had obtained permission from GLNY to publish this chorus in its series for mixed voices.[30] In that same month, Kramer wrote to George Sjöblom with the news that Galaxy had plans to release various choral versions of "Onward, ye Peoples!" Included would be "two versions for mixed chorus—one, a large festival version, the other a simple, more practical one."[31] In addition, Galaxy was interested in having Sibelius arrange this piece for orchestra. To that end, Kramer needed Sjöblom to communicate this to Sibelius in Finnish, including specific recommendations about the instrumentation.[32] After an exchange of letters between Sjöblom and Sibelius brought the response Galaxy had been seeking, Kramer wrote directly to Sibelius, reiterating the instrumentation requirements and suggesting other changes. For example, Kramer wanted the key changed from C major to A major and the time signature from 3/2 to 3/4. He suggested that the single chord at the beginning of No. 6 be replaced with either "a few measures of introduction" or "a brief fanfare" and that the lower instruments (double bass and violoncello) reinforce the initial notes of the measures carrying the main theme. This last request was made because the rhythmic pulse of the accompaniment for the main theme needed reinforcement in order to be audible to the chorus.[33]

Among the many autograph manuscripts and sketches related to opus 113 that are extant in the Helsinki University Library is a fair copy of Sibelius's 1938

---

30    The document which permitted Galaxy to publish an arrangement of item no. 6 as a non-Masonic choral composition is in the "Sibelius" file at LML. The original bears the signature of Charles Johnson and the seal of the Grand Lodge of the State of New York, but it is not dated. A date of 13 April 1938 was subsequently typed at the top of the document and that of 14 April 1938 was stamped in the upper right corner to indicate receipt of the document at LML. That this document was drawn up several weeks prior to 13 April is evident from references made to it in a letter written by A. Walter Kramer to George Sjöblom (4 April 1938). S. v. the "Sibelius Family Collection 35/94," National Archives, Helsinki. Excerpts from the Kramer letter were provided to the author by Fabian Dahlström.

31    Letter from A. Walter Kramer to George Sjöblom (14 April 1938) in the "Sibelius Family Collection 36/94," National Archives of Finland.

32    Letter from A. Walter Kramer to George Sjöblom (14 April 1938) in the "Sibelius Family Collection 36/94," National Archives of Finland. Walter Kramer served as editor-in-chief of *Musical America* before joning the Galaxy Music Corp. as Managing Director in May 1936. Judging from the amount of correspondence Kramer had with Sibelius, he appears to have been the principal negotiator for the non-Masonic publications related to opus 113.

33    Letter from A. Walter Kramer to Sibelius (1 June 1938) in the "Sibelius Family Collection 36/94." National Archives of Finland. When Hugh Ross conducted the chorus for the Preview concert in May, he had difficulty holding the chorus together because the singers could not hear the accompaniment that was scored in a high register.

orchestration of No. 6, entitled "Processional" (K. 1197). The score is in the key of A major, has a tempo mark of "*Largamente e maestoso,*" and is scored for a large orchestra: 2 flutes, 2 clarinets in A, 2 bassoons, 4 horns in E, 2 trumpets in E, 3 trombones, 1 tuba, timpani, violins I and II, alto (viola), cello, and contrabass.[34] The choral parts are not included in the score, although two staves (labeled "Coro" for SATB) are reserved for them. Sibelius purposely left those staves blank because he had been informed by Sjöblom that Galaxy planned to issue "Processional" in both orchestral and choral-orchestral versions. For this latter version, Channing Lefebvre created an arrangement for SATB chorus.[35]

The most striking difference between Sibelius's 1938 orchestral score and the 1936 edition of No. 6 for voice and keyboard accompaniment is the addition of an eight-measure introduction, written in the style of a majestic fanfare. As mentioned above, Kramer had asked Sibelius to consider making this compositional change. So effective was this introductory addition to the original piece that these eight measures appear in all the various vocal and instrumental versions of *Onward, Ye Peoples!* published by Galaxy for non-Masonic use.[36]

Lefebvre's arrangement for mixed chorus wedded to Sibelius's orchestral accompaniment was first presented 11 May 1939 at the May Festival of the University of Michigan in Ann Arbor. Six months later, on October 6th, it was performed at the Worcester (MA) Music Festival.[37] Lefebvre's concept of how the original solo vocal part of No. 6 should be transformed into a choral piece

---

34  For a comparison with the instrumentation used by Funtek, see chapter five.

35  From 1922 until 1941, Channing Lefebvre was organist at Trinity Church in New York City. He also served as an "in house" arranger for Galaxy Music Corporation. After 1941 he became Director of Music at St. Paul's School in Concord, NH.

36  Upon receipt of Sibelius's orchestral score, Kramer wrote to the composer and thanked him for the "truly marvelous instrumentation" and for "having prepared so attractive an introduction." This letter (28 October 1938) is in the "Sibelius Family Collection 36/94," National Archives of Finland. *Onward, Ye Peoples!* is how the title of the non-Masonic versions was printed by Galaxy Music Corp., whereas the opening line of the vocal versions is correctly printed as "Onward, ye Peoples!" with a lower case "y." In the Masonic editions of opus 113, "Onward, ye Brethren" is the title as well as the opening line for this piece.

37  Sibelius completed the orchestral score by October 1938 and Galaxy published the Lefebvre/Sibelius version in February 1939. Printed on the back cover of the published score was an announcement of the first two performances that were planned for May and October of 1939. See also "A Brace of Festivals," *The New York Times* (23 April 1939):X, 7; "80th Worcester Fete," *The New York Times* (1 Oct 1939):IX,6; and Straus, "Sibelius Score" (1948), where these same performances are mentioned.

differed noticeably from Kernochan's choral arrangement. He worked on the premise that the melody should be given a prominent position. If it could not be sung by the uppermost vocal part in the full chorus passage, then it would be given to a single vocal part, with the other vocal parts remaining silent or providing an accompanying role. In other words, he wanted to avoid having the melody buried in an inner part, as had been done in Kernochan's arrangement for the Masonic edition. As a result, Lefebvre's choral writing incorporates a variety of textures ranging from a single vocal part to all four parts singing together.

Galaxy negotiated a separate, royalty-generating, contract with Sibelius for the non-Masonic versions of No. 6 from opus 113 and within a few years more than 100,000 copies of *Onward, Ye Peoples!* were sold. According to at least one person's opinion expressed in a published report, Sibelius netted more in royalties from the sale of this single item than he had "ever received for his music from either Breitkopf & Härtel or any other publishers."[38] That may be a bit of an exaggeration, but in the period from 1939 to 1949 Sibelius earned approximately $5,000 in royalties from this one composition. The composer's contract specified that his royalties be divided equally between himself and the orphanage founded in his name, but Sibelius instructed Galaxy to send his royalty checks directly to the Grand Lodge of Finland, where a fund had been established for the benefit of The Sibelius Home for Children.[39]

Two weeks after the May Day Preview, Downes sent a letter to Sibelius with a detailed description of the afternoon concert. He begins the letter with these words: "I think you would have been thrilled if you had heard your hymn sung at the close of our afternoon Pageant of the 'Preview' of the World's Fair."[40] Although Downes does not mention the work by name, there is no question

---

38   Ostman and Rutzy, "25 Years of Finlandia Masonic Club." A copy of the article is in SFC, but the source from which it comes is not indicated nor is the date of publication.

39   Some of the royalty statements issued to Sibelius by the Galaxy Music Corp. for his non-Masonic publications from opus 113, dating from 1939 through the 1970s, are extant in the "Sibelius" file at LML and in the "Sibelius Family Collection 36/94" in the National Archives of Finland. At the conclusion of World War II, royalties earned between 1939 and 1948 were paid by Galaxy in a lump sum to the Grand Lodge of Finland on behalf of Sibelius.

40   The letter, dated 15 May 1938, is quoted in Goss, *Jean Sibelius and Olin Downes*, 203.

that the hymn was "Onward, ye Peoples!" That notwithstanding, there has been at least one claim that the hymn performed was "Finlandia."[41]

The performance of music by Sibelius at the Preview concert in May of 1938 was but a foretaste of what Downes had planned as the "prelude" to the official opening of the World's Fair in April of 1939. The work Downes most wanted to be premiered at the fair was Sibelius's Eighth Symphony.[42] When it became known that the composer would not be forthcoming with a new symphony, Downes had to formulate other plans to showcase the composer's music. In December 1938, after Sibelius's 70th birthday had been celebrated with the usual flurry of concerts and notes of congratulations, Downes sent Sibelius a telegram asking if he would consent to conduct one or more of his works for a round-the-world broadcast on New Year's Day. Sibelius lost no time in giving his response. He immediately cabled Downes and agreed to conduct his music with the Helsinki Philharmonic Orchestra. On Christmas Day Downes cabled his thanks to Sibelius and then used the occasion to wish the Sibelius family holiday greetings.[43]

Finland was the first nation to accept an invitation to participate in the "Salute to Nations" prelude event and therefore was given the honor of presenting the initial program. It took place in Radio City Music Hall on 1 January 1939 and was broadcast worldwide. The program opened with greetings from some of Finland's government officials, followed by the broadcast performance from Helsinki of the orchestral versions of *Finlandia* and *Andante festivo*. This marked the first international broadcast for Sibelius as a conductor.[44] The Finnish program concluded with national songs sung by the Finlandia Male

---

41  Ibid., 115. *The New York Times* correctly reported that the hymn sung was "Onward, ye Peoples!" (2 May 1938):19.

42  As early as 15 October 1938, Sibelius had personally written a response to A. Walter Kramer's suggestion that Galaxy publish his Eighth Symphony. He told Kramer the work was promised long ago to the firm of Wilhelm Hansen in Copenhagen. S. v. letters exchanged between Kramer and Sibelius (2 Sept 1938 and 15 Oct 1938) in the "Sibelius Family Collection 36/94," National Archives of Finland.

43  Goss, 205, letter no. 43.

44  Coincidentally, this was also the very last time Sibelius appeared as a conductor. For that reason, the broadcast tapes from the 1 January 1939 event were highly prized and duplicate copies were made by the Finnish Broadcasting Company from the master recording. Between the 1940s and the 1990s, recordings purported to have been made from the 1939 broadcast tapes were marketed worldwide. Not until the spring of 1995, however, did anyone realize that those recordings of *Andante festivo* were under the baton of another conductor. A recording (CD) of the original 1939 concert has now been released and it offers "the only

Chorus, a group that was also to perform for the next "Salute to Nations" on 8 January 1939. "Salute to Nations" programs were aired on each successive Sunday until the fair's opening day in April.

At the conclusion of the performance of Sibelius's orchestral music, Finland's Foreign Minister, Eljas Erkko, addressed the audience. In the course of his remarks, he made clear Finland's willingness to advance the cause of peace and prosperity throughout the world and singled out Sibelius as the one person who, through his music, had effectively communicated that idea to Americans.[45] Erkko's remarks were quoted in one of two articles related to this "Salute to Nations" concert, which appeared in the *The New York Times* on 2 January 1939. The other article, printed on the editorial page, praised the choice of Finland and its foremost composer to open the event. The article then noted that Sibelius's music reached a far greater audience than he might have imagined, for the broadcast was heard by an international audience that spanned the globe.[46]

It was also in May of 1939 that the various pavilions of the New York World's Fair held special ceremonies marking their official opening to the public. The ceremony for Finland's pavilion included the reading of a congratulatory telegram from Sibelius and remarks by the mayor of New York City. The American public had already become aware of Finland through the life and music of its world famous composer. Now it had a rare opportunity to gain a closer look at Finland's history, culture, and natural resources in this uniquely designed structure, described as a "Symphony in Wood."[47]

Shortly after the Preview concert, Marshall Kernochan drew up for Sibelius a publication contract "with provision for phonograph recordings" that he wanted George Sjöblom to review before it was sent to Finland. Although the work under contract was not specified in Kernochan's letter of 26 May 1938 to Sjöblom, it obviously concerned "Onward, ye Peoples!"[48] Kernochan wanted to send the contract to Sibelius "as soon as possible so that we can get it back signed and go ahead with the preparation of the various versions."

document we have of Sibelius conducting his own music." See Antero Karttune, "True and False *Andante Festivo*," *Finnish Music Quarterly* (4/95):57–58.

45   See "Finland Salutes US in Broadcast," *The New York Times* (2 Jan 1939):2, as well as an excerpt of Erkko's remarks on pages 72–73 of the first edition of this book..

46   See "Finland's Voice," *The New York Times* (2 Jan 1939):22.

47   "Symphony in Wood of Finns Has Debut," *The New York Times* (5 May 1939):18.

48   Letter from Marshall Kernochan to George Sjöblom (26 May 1938) in the SFC.

Since Kernochan did not know Finnish, he often relied on native speakers such as George Sjöblom to communicate with Sibelius on behalf of Galaxy Music Corporation. In this instance, Kernochan wanted a letter sent with the contract, which would explain to the composer that Galaxy was "more than anxious to have him receive as much as possible on this work of his which we are so proud to publish."[49]

The urgency expressed in Kernochan's letter to have the contract signed and returned to Galaxy did not translate into an immediate response from Sibelius. When more than a month passed without any communication from Järvenpää, the president of Galaxy, A Walter Kramer, decided to again enlist the aid of George Sjöblom who was vacationing in Finland with his family. Kramer knew that Sjöblom had scheduled a visit with Sibelius and decided to have him remind the composer to sign the contract. To that end, Kramer sent the following telegram to Sjöblom in Helsinki on 27 July 1938:

KINDLY SEE SIBELIUS AND ADVISE HIM TO SIGN CONTRACT ONWARD YE PEOPLES THANKS REGARDS/ KRAMER GALAXY[50]

Sibelius subsequently signed the contract and Galaxy was able to publish a number of different versions of "Onward, ye Peoples!" in 1939, all of them covered by both American and international copyrights.[51] No sooner were the

---

49  Ibid. In the final paragraph of this letter, Kernochan writes: "We are this week going to get hold of the original Finnish text of 'Onward, ye Peoples!' and I may be obliged to consult you in regard to the spelling of various words if the manuscript is not clear." This statement is a bit puzzling because the "original Finnish text" for No. 6 was supplied along with the Swedish text of Rydberg when the manuscript was presented to the GLNY in 1935. Therefore Kernochan must be referring to a Finnish version of a non-Masonic text that could be performed by Finnish choral groups in the United States. The reference may be to a publication in Finland of "Onward, ye Peoples!" with Finnish lyrics by George (Yrjö) Sjöblom, which in the TEOSTO listing of Sibelius's works is assigned the number 0401C.

50  This telegram is in SFC.

51  These 1939 versions included arrangements by Channing Lefebvre for SSA and SA (©1 March 1939), special piano and organ accompaniments for the choral versions (©13 April 1939), organ solo (©28 April 1939), and the rental of instrumental parts for the orchestral arrangement by Sibelius (©10 April 1939). Since Sibelius's version for symphonic orchestra was only available "for hire," Galaxy decided (with the composer's permission) to have the full orchestral score arranged for small orchestra and in this form could make it available for purchase. So popular did this composition become, it was soon subjected to pirated

Galaxy editions on the market than Sibelius was contemplating whether or not to sign another publication contract for "Onward, ye Peoples!"—this time with the music publishing firm of Wilhelm Hansen in Copenhagen. In a letter dated 6 May 1939, Sibelius wrote in Swedish to Hansen and told him he had not decided whether or not to publish the piece in Europe.[52]

The successful arrangement of "Onward, ye Peoples!" with orchestral accompaniment may have motivated Wäinö Sola to suggest a similar arrangement be made of the entire 'Musique réligieuse." Sola also suggested that a recording be made of the orchestrated version with himself as the vocal soloist. He reasoned that if such a recording were available, it could be used whenever the "Grand Singer" or "Grand Organist" could not perform the ritual music for SSL. Even more important than the practical application of having a recording would have been its preservation of an authentic interpretation of opus 113.

In 1940 Sola shared his ideas about opus 113 with the Grand Master of SSL, Juho Kousmanan, who readily agreed the proposal for orchestrating the accompaniment was worth pursuing with Sibelius.[53] Sola was confident that Sibelius would give his consent; he was equally confident that Sibelius would decline to do the orchestration by himself, if for no other reason than that he had difficulty controlling the motions of his right hand. Sibelius suffered from some sort of tremor in that hand.

Tawaststjerna, in his biography of the composer, subtly calls attention to this tremor in his account of Sibelius's 1914 visit to the Norfolk Festival in Connecticut. He describes a typical morning for Sibelius while he stayed throughout the festival with his hosts, Carl and Ellen Battell Stoeckel, at their estate known as the White House: "As on all the mornings he spent in the White House, Sibelius rose fairly early and was shaved by a barber, specially engaged for the purpose at his request." In a footnote to this sentence, Tawaststjerna adds: "His tremor probably prompted this request."[54] This is

---

publication and performance. S. v. letters (15 March 1939, 16 Sept 1940) in the "Sibelius Family Collection 36/94" in the National Archives of Finland that documents one such incident.

52  Fabian Dahlström saw this letter when it was in the archives of Edition Wilhelm Hansen and was able to share the information with the author. The letter is currently in a private collection.

53  Marvia, *Sibeliuksen Rituaalimusiikki*, 91.

54  Tawaststjerna (Layton, trans.), II, 274n2.

one of the few times that any mention of the tremor has found its way into print, even though this peculiar condition of Sibelius's hand had been noticed by others who had personal contact with the composer. They included Wäinö Sola, Einari Marvia, and John Kernochan, son of Marshall Kernochan, who visited Ainola in 1939.[55]

Sola proved to be correct in his assumptions. Sibelius declined the offer to create the orchestration, even though he was in favor of the idea. Instead, he gave Sola permission to commission Leo Funtek, a conductor of international reputation, to orchestrate the eight sections of the ritual music in his place. Funds to pay Funtek were donated by a Mason who wished to remain anonymous. This donor asked that the orchestral score become the property of SSL and that SSL make the orchestral score available to other lodges for performance. Some additional funding also came from a special Sibelius fund that had been established at the St. John's Lodge in Finland.[56]

The orchestral arrangement by Leo Funtek was completed 21 June 1940 but never published, which perhaps accounts for the very few performances the work has enjoyed up to the present time. The first was given in Helsinki on 12 December 1958, when the tenor Jorma Huttunen sang with the Helsinki Philharmonic Orchestra, conducted by Tauno Hannikainen.[57] The second performance in Finland occurred in 1987. This time it was with the Radio Finland Orchestra. There have been at least three other performances of Funtek's arrangement: two in Germany in 1971 and 1977and one in the United States in 1995.[58] Although recordings have been made of the various versions of opus 113 with a tenor soloist accompanied by either organ or orchestra, none were made with Wäinö Sola, the principal interpreter of the score for almost three decades.

---

55    John Kernochan shared this information with the author in 1995. Wäinö Sola, in a letter to Marshall Kernochan (20 Feb 1952), mentioned the difficulties Sibelius had taking care of correspondence because "some times his hands are trembling." A copy of Sola's letter is in the National Archives of Finland.

56    Marvia, op. cit. 91.

57    Huttunen substituted for Antti Koskinen, who was ill. Fabian Dahlström kindly provided the author with a copy of the 1958 program. See also Marvia, op. cit., 183.

58    Marvia, op. cit., 92. The 1995 performance was given on 22 October in the Masonic Hall of the GLNY as part of a concert program celebrating the 130th anniversary of Sibelius's birth. The performance was recorded and issued as part of a commemorative 2-CD set. For a discussion of the Funtek score, see the next chapter.

# CHAPTER FIVE

## LEO FUNTEK'S ORCHESTRATION OF OPUS 113

There are few Masonic lodges in Finland or the United States where a performance of Leo Funtek's orchestrated version of opus 113 (C-113-40), completed in 1940, could or would take place; yet, it is precisely this version of the original eight pieces that captures the true essence of Sibelius's music. Many lodges are equipped with excellent organs for ritual use, but no matter how fine these instruments may be, they can give only a faint hint of the variegated timbres and colors possible from a full symphonic orchestra. So naturally does the keyboard accompaniment adapt to orchestral scoring, it suggests that the composer himself must have conceived the work in this form.[1] No wonder Sibelius vented his wrath on the harmonium at Suomi Lodge No. 1 when it could not measure up to his expectations of volume for his *fortissimo* passages. He in all likelihood had in mind the full orchestral sound that the Funtek score brings forth.

---

1   In a lecture delivered by Wäinö Sola in the late 1950s, he mentions that there is a note written in the margin in the 1927 manuscript of the opening piece of opus 113 that reads: "Johdanto loosin avaukseen, Adagio orkesterille" (Introduction to the opening of the lodge, Adagio to the orchestra). Since this is the only instance that the word "orkesterille" comes up in connection with the original version of opus 113, Marvia has interpreted this as a hint that Sibelius actually intended the music to be played by an orchestra. Perhaps this singular mention of "orkesterille" also caused Arthur Sharp to mistakenly mention in his lecture of 1961 that "'Musique réligieuse'…was first made for small orchestra and later fully orchestrated." See Marvia, *Sibeliuksen Rituaalimusiikki*, 25; Sharp, "Sibelius's Masonic Ritual Music," 5.

As was mentioned in the previous chapter, Funtek's orchestration has never been published. Therefore the following remarks are based solely on a photocopy of the manuscript of the conductor's score.[2] On the title page, Funtek has written "Rituaali-musiikki (1927) op. 113," followed by "Ork. sov. Leo Funtek."[3] In addition to Funtek's signature, Sibelius's signature also is written at the top of the same page, giving tacit approval to Funtek's work. Since there is no record of any performance of Funtek's orchestral arrangement, public or private, until 1958, it is presumed that Sibelius never had the opportunity to hear this version of opus 113.

How much interaction occurred between Funtek and Sibelius during the period when the orchestral arrangement was being written is not known. The score, however, yields evidence that there must have been some communication, if not with Sibelius directly, then with Sola as an intermediary, for it does not reproduce verbatim the music as it was written in 1927 or printed in 1936. Interestingly, most of the changes that make their appearance in the Funtek score were subsequently adopted by Sibelius for the 1948 manuscript version of opus 113 sent to New York.

Funtek was born in Ljubljana (Slovenia) in 1885 and educated at both the University and Conservatory of Leipzig. In 1906 he moved to Helsinki to conduct the city's Philharmonic Orchestra and ended up spending the rest of his life in Finland, becoming one of its most celebrated citizens. Over the years he distinguished himself as a teacher of violin and conducting at the Sibelius Academy in Helsinki, as a conductor of the Finnish Opera orchestra, and most importantly as an orchestral arranger. He has been especially lauded for his orchestrated version of Mussorgsky's *Pictures at an Exhibition*.[4]

Funtek's version of opus 113 requires a large orchestra: flutes, oboes, clarinets, bassoons, horns, trumpets, trombones, timpani (triangle, cymbals, tamtam), glockenspiel, harp, and strings (3/3/2/2/1). Seldom, however, does Funtek call on the full complement of these orchestral forces. For example, the opening piece (No. 1) is scored for woodwinds and strings, but the woodwinds and the contrabass do not enter until after the fermata at measure 14, from which point they continue through the end of the piece. In this particular instance,

---

2   The copy consulted was sent from SSL for the October 1995 performance sponsored by the Sixth Manhattan District of the GLNY. Since no orchestral parts were sent from Finland, they were created from this same copy of the conductor's score.
3   The Finnish abbreviations stand for "adapted for orchestra."
4   S. v. "Funtek, Leo," *The New Grove Dictionary of Music*, III, 525.

Funtek makes audible the structure of the music through his handling of the orchestration.

As mentioned above, Funtek's score sometimes contains a reading that was eventually to find its way into a later revised edition of opus 113. One such example can be found in No. 1 in the notation of measure 18, which offers a reading similar to that in the 1950 edition, where only the lowest note is tied over from the previous measure.

In No. 2, Funtek limits the scoring to woodwinds and contrabass. The resulting timbre imitates the sound of an organ and thereby evokes a feeling of the sacred. The vocal part (with Finnish lyrics) is supported, but never overpowered, by the instruments. Sibelius wanted to make a slight change in measure 13 of this piece from what he had written in 1927, but when that change was incorporated into MS-113-48, it produced an error that also affected measure 13 in the 1950 edition. The Funtek score shows how the revision should have been made: the voice and accompaniment sustain their respective notes for the full value of measure 12 and then initiate a new phrase simultaneously in measure 13. In other words, the B-flat in the lowest sounding part (the bassoon) of measure 12 is not supposed to be tied over into measure 13. Instead, the B-flat is to be sounded anew, not only in the bassoon, but also in the contrabass part which enters in measure 13 for the first time.

Not all of the revisions Sibelius wanted for the second printed edition of opus 113 are introduced in Funtek's score. To give but one example, in measure 21 of the 1936 edition the voice enters on the first beat of the measure with a dotted whole note. This same reading obtains in Funtek's score, but in MS-113-48 Sibelius decided to begin measure 21 with two half-note rests, delaying the entry of the voice until the third beat of the measure.

The scoring for the instrumental section of No. 3 consists of clarinets, bassoons, violas (divisi) and cellos (divisi). Clarinet I and viola I carry the melodic material in a register appropriate to these instruments, the same register Sibelius adopted for the whole of No. 3 in MS-113-48. In other words, the musical material is positioned an octave lower than it was in the 1936 edition. Did Funtek's scoring influence the revision that occurs in MS-113-48 or was his scoring made in response to the wishes of the composer? Given the number of revisions incorporated into the 1940 score, the evidence would seem to suggest that Sibelius had decided on all of them almost a decade before they appear in MS-113-48.

No. 4 has three distinct sections—"Marcia," "Trio I," and "Trio II"—and the orchestration chosen by Funtek for each is equally distinct. The woodwinds, one horn in F, and the triangle are used for the "Marcia." To these instruments, Funtek adds all the strings for "Trio I." When the voice enters in "Trio II," the scoring is reduced to one flute, one clarinet, one bassoon, with violins and violas playing "con sordino." The overall effect achieved is one of lightness in texture.

The introspective mood of No. 5 is greatly enhanced by Funtek's orchestral arrangement. So effective is his scoring for this piece, it is difficult to conceive of any other interpretation for the accompaniment. Funtek uses violins I and II (divisi) and a single viola, all playing "con sordino," for the first verse, and then to these instruments he introduces a piccolo to play the sustained dotted whole notes that Sibelius added for the second verse. The other-worldly atmosphere of this piece recalls a similar effect created in Sibelius's Sixth Symphony.

Although no part is included for the cello in No. 5, Funtek has written the word "cello" in the opening measure above the vocal staff. Either he wanted this instrument to play in unison with the singer to reinforce the seamless quality of the vocal line or he was suggesting this instrument as a substitute for the vocal part. A similar situation occurs in several of the other numbers where the name of an instrument (or instruments) is written above the vocal part. In most cases, the additions do not seem to be in Funtek's hand.

The Funtek arrangement of No. 6 is quite different from the orchestral version Sibelius made for Galaxy in 1938. It is in the key of F and is designed to accompany a solo voice, not a chorus. Therefore the scoring is more modest, consisting of woodwinds, horns, and strings. For the most part Funtek reserves the full scoring for climactic sections, such as the setting of the word "Salem" in measures 58–59; yet, even here the dynamic level desired is only *forte*. In the corresponding climactic sections in the 1938 vocal-orchestral and 1950 vocal-organ versions of this piece, Sibelius wanted them played *fortissimo*. Not only does Funtek restrain the dynamic level in No. 6, he also reinterprets where the climactic points should occur. Most notable in this regard is the way Funtek concludes No. 6. The full orchestra accompanies measures 66–70 and then the scoring is reduced to strings playing *piano* in measures 71–74. At measure 75, the full orchestra (minus oboes) is called for again, but this time the instruments are scored in their lowest registers and are playing *piano*. Only the voice, which in this version has the octave leap to the final word "Salem," is allowed to gently soar above the accompaniment.

It may seem out of character to find timpani, glockenspiel, cymbals, trumpets, and horns in the scoring for No. 7, which offers a very pastoral setting of Rydberg's poetry; yet, those are the very instruments Funtek has included along with woodwinds, strings, and the harp.[5] His particular arrangement, however, is very sparing in the use of the brass and percussion. Moreover, when these instruments do appear in the section that is borrowed from Sibelius's *Andante festivo*, they are playing *pianissimo* and therefore do not intrude on the delicate texture of the piece. Here and in No. 6, the lyrics are given in both Finnish and Swedish.

Funtek waits until No. 8, the "Marche funèbre," to engage the full orchestra (minus the harp). The brass and woodwinds take center stage in the opening section where the reference to the chorale melody from "Herzlich thut mich verlangen" is strongly emphasized. His orchestral arrangement draws attention to the essential sameness of the motivic structure. It also provides the means to effectively execute the rhythmic aspect of the piece. Whereas the organ lacks the crisp attack needed for the repeated triplet figures, brass and percussion are able to provide the desired contrast with the melodic motives centered in the strings and upper woodwinds. The structure of this piece is the same as in the 1927 and 1936 versions, with a repetition of measures 1–40 followed by a brief coda. It is in the final six measures of the coda that the dynamic level which Sibelius had envisioned when he first composed this piece is achieved, as every instrument is asked to play triple *forte*.

Although it is not necessary to perform Funtek's score in the order in which the pieces are numbered, it seems obvious from the orchestration that Funtek intended the music to be heard in this sequence. That having been said, it should be pointed out that his orchestral arrangement is equally effective when the pieces are heard in a different order. For example, when the Funtek version

---

5    The scoring of Sibelius's Fourth Symphony also includes the glockenspiel (as confirmed by the recently discovered orchestral parts used at the premiere). Since this instrument appears in Mozart's *Die Zauberflöte*, there has been an attempt on the part of some scholars to link Sibelius's use of the instrument with the Masonic symbolism in the opera. Such an interpretation, however, is difficult to defend. Nevertheless, Funtek's brief inclusion of the glockenspiel in No. 7 may indeed have had Masonic implications, given the fact that Freemasonry, along with the ritual use of Mozart's music, was well established in Finland by this date.

was performed in the Grand Hall of the GLNY in October 1995, the pieces were heard in this order: numbers 1 through 5, 8, 7, and 6. This New York premiere, with Martti Miettinen (soloist) and the New York Metamorphoses Orchestra, was recorded live, and it is this version that is now available on a compact disc. This means that listeners are not hearing the orchestral score played in the sequence in which it was most likely conceived by Funtek. Those who attended the New York concert or have listened to the recording based on that performance have been surprised how the orchestrated version not only enriches the original vocal-organ version but also transforms it into a work that is so distinctively recognizable as being by Sibelius.

# CHAPTER SIX

## THE POETIC SOURCES FOR
## *MASONIC RITUAL MUSIC*

### Sibelius and His Views of Religion

The opening words of a statement concerning Freemasonry and religion prepared by the Masonic Information Center in 1993 read as follows:

> Freemasonry is not a religion, nor is it a substitute for religion. It requires of its members belief in God as part of the obligation of every responsible adult, but advocates no sectarian faith or practice. Masonic ceremonies include prayers, both traditional and extempore, to reaffirm each individual's dependence on God and to seek divine guidance.... Masonry believes in religious freedom and that the relationship between the individual and God is personal, private, and sacred.[1]

It does not take a stretch of imagination to see how these words, had they been written a century earlier, could have spoken to the heart and soul of Sibelius. If Masonry had not been banned from Finland between 1822 and 1922, he might well have found interest in the fraternity long before his fifty-sixth birthday.

Jean Sibelius was born on 8 December 1865 in Hämeelinna, a town some 30 or 40 miles north of Helsinki. He grew up in a home where chamber music was

---

1   "Freemasonry and Religion," Masonic Information Center (Dec 1993).

very much a part of his family's life: he played violin, his brother Christian played cello, and his sister Linda played the piano. Sibelius's home town had neither a theater nor a resident orchestra, and therefore professional entertainment was limited to the touring ensembles. As for local entertainment, it came primarily in the form of concerts by male-voice quartets whose repertoire consisted principally of Scandinavian and German part-songs.[2] Perhaps Sibelius's early acquaintance with male quartets influenced his noticeable preference for this combination of voices (TTBB) in his choral music.

There was, of course, a rich heritage of music in the local church, but Sibelius did not hear much of it, for his attendance at services was very infrequent. In fact, the only time he could be counted on to worship with the rest of his family was at Christmas, an occasion that was said to afford him "affectionate memories … later in life."[3] Tawaststjerna has interpreted Sibelius's apparent detachment from organized religion as an indication that another spiritual force was operative in the composer's life:

> The nearest thing to religious feeling that he experienced was his awe of Nature. His concept of God was pantheistic, closely related in feeling with Rydberg in his poem "På verandan vid haver" ("On the balcony by the sea").[4]

Admittedly, Sibelius did not look at nature in an ordinary and mundane way; he lived in and through nature. It enveloped his entire being, so much so that his brother-in-law, Arvid Järnefelt (1861–1932), used to describe him as "a creature of nature."[5] Others who knew Sibelius well were equally cognizant of the close relationship that existed between his experiences of nature and his musical creativity.[6] Ernest Newman recalled a conversation in which Sibelius told him "that the origins and the working-out of his musical thoughts were determined by mental images … from definite impressions of nature and

---

2   Tawaststjerna (Layton, trans.), *Sibelius, 1865–1905*, I, 21–22.
3   Ibid., 20.
4   Ibid.
5   Ibid., 46.
6   Sibelius's "Ensam i dunkla skogarnas fann," a choral work written in 1888 while he was a student in the Helsinki Music Institute, underscores with its opening phrase "Along in the dark forest's clasp I make my lonesome way" (as translated from the Swedish by William Jewson) how the composer himself may have experienced the awesomeness of the natural world.

of human life." Adolf Paul (1863–1943) found these images were Sibelius's "external promptings" that produced "corresponding impressions on his ear" and hence, musical ideas.[7] A glimpse at the kind of images Sibelius associated with his music can be seen in a pencil drawing he made in the late 1880s to accompany one of his early chamber works.[8]

Nowhere is Sibelius's love of nature more revealing than in the entries he made in his diary and in a series of conversations he had in the 1930s with Karl Ekman, who wrote a "memoir" type of biography of the composer. He told Ekman that when World War I caused him to be isolated from the music capitals of Europe, his diary entries show how he did his "best to forget the evil of the times" by "studying nature" around him. For example, his enthusiastic welcome of the first days of spring is captured in this diary entry for 18 April 1917: "A wonderful spring day, spring and life. The earth smells, mutes and fortissimo. An extraordinary light, reminiscent of a haze in August."[9] Similar reflections of his joyous reception of spring repeatedly occur in Sibelius's music, as in the 1894 spring song for orchestra, *Vårsång* (*La tristisse du printemps*), and the 1918 cantata for chorus and orchestra, *Oma maa*, in praise of the lengthening nights of light in Finland.

In 1940 when Paul Sjöblom and Martti Similä visited Sibelius in his temporary residence in Helsinki, they were reminded of how great a role nature had always played in the composer's life. Sibelius was living in an apartment on the third floor of a six-story building from which he could gaze out on pine trees and flowers in the yard below, and "a short distance farther" he could see "a wooded path, leading to lonely paths by the sea." Inside the apartment there were other reminders that the natural world held a special fascination for him. In addition to the flowers arrayed along the windows, a large oil painting that hung in a prominent place in the living room drew the observer into a "wild winter landscape." It was painted by a neighbor in Järvenpää and, according to Sjöblom, was such a favorite of the composer that it went with him wherever his "home" happened to be.[10]

---

7    Ekman, *Jean Sibelius: His Life and Personality*, viii.
8    This drawing for the 1887 Quartet for Piano, Violin, Cello and Harmonium is illustrated in H. E. Johnson, *Sibelius*, 15.
9    Ekman, *Jean Sibelius*, 243–44.
10   Paul Sjöblom, " An Interview with Sibelius. The Finnish Old Master Talks of Music and War," 34.

It was not merely the incredible beauty and peacefulness of Finland's natural environment that may have moved Sibelius toward a concept of God that was pantheistic. One of New York State's own natural wonders engendered a similar response from the composer during his first and only sojourn in this country. He visited Niagara Falls in 1914 as a guest of Carl Stoeckel, and afterwards his host wrote these words in a diary preserved at Yale University:

> As [Sibelius] viewed the spectacle, there was an expression on his face of one who is experiencing profoundly religious emotions.... he might have inherited the old Scandinavian feelings of the great phenomena of nature being the dwelling places of divinities.[11]

Those "dwelling places of divinities" are the subject of *Tapiola*, a tone poem that represents the pinnacle of Sibelius's orchestral writing. The title for *Tapiola* is derived from the name of the realm ruled by Tapio, the mythological Finnish god of the forest. Sibelius alludes to Tapio in his preface to the score: "Widespread they stand, the Northland's dusky forests, ancient, mysterious, brooding savage dreams; and within them dwells the forest's mighty God, and woodsprites in the gloom weave magic secrets."[12]

*Tapiola* was the fulfillment of a commission that the composer received in 1925 from Harry Harkness Flagler, president of the Philharmonic-Symphony Society of New York. It is likely that the idea for the commission originated with Walter Damrosch, conductor of the Society's orchestra, which premiered the work on 26 December 1926 in New York City. Damrosch had met Sibelius at the 1914 Norfolk Festival when the composer conducted the premiere of *Oceanides* along with several of his other works. The performance of *Tapiola* took place in the auditorium of the Mecca Temple located at 310 West 56th Street. On the same program was Beethoven's Fifth Symphony and Gershwin's F major Piano Concerto, with George Gershwin as soloist.

In a favorable review of the concert, the music of the tone poem was likened to a solitary figure silhouetted against a dimly lighted background of nature.[13] Other reviews of Sibelius's music have also defined the compositional process in

---

11    Stoeckel, "Some Reflections of the Visit of Sibelius to America in 1914," 76. This is a reprint from the Stoeckel diary.
12    Wood, "The Miscellaneous Orchestral and Theatre Music," 40.
13    See "Music," *The New York Times* (27 Dec 1926):20.

terms of nature as experienced by a solitary figure. A case in point is a review of his symphonic music by Olin Downes, music critic for *The New York Times*.[14]

In the twelve-year interval between the premieres of *Oceanides* and *Tapiola*, Sibelius brought forth his Fifth, Sixth, and Seventh Symphonies, incidental orchestral music for *Jedermann* and *The Tempest*, and *Väinön virsi* for chorus and orchestra—each an important work in its own right. But it was in *Tapiola* that Sibelius wed his orchestral mastery with his love of nature and Finnish mythology.

In Ekman's biography, there are brief glimpses of Sibelius's concept of a divine power at work in his life. In a letter written in May of 1918, the composer expressed the belief that his last three symphonies were "more in the nature of professions of faith" than in his other works. That the form of these symphonies did not exactly end up as Sibelius had originally planned was explained to Ekman in these words:

> The final form of one's work is, indeed, dependent on powers that are stronger than oneself. Later on, one can substantiate this or that, but on the whole one is merely a tool. This wonderful logic—let us call it God—that governs a work of art is the forcing power.[15]

Ekman records another interesting episode that occurred in the fall of 1911, when Sibelius was in Europe and heard for the first time a performance of Anton Bruckner's Symphony in B major. Sibelius expressed his impressions of this work in a letter with these words:

> ... it moved me to tears. For a long time afterwards I was completely enraptured. What a strange profound spirit, formed by religiousness! And this profound religiousness we have abolished in our own country as something no longer in harmony with our time.[16]

Just what Sibelius meant by "profound religiousness" is not revealed in the Ekman biography, but the author does quote Sibelius as saying (ca. 1915) that he "found it impossible to define a religion—least of all in words. But perhaps

---

14   See Downes, "Sibelius at Seventy," *The New York Times* (8 Dec 1935):22, as well as an excerpt from his review on page 140 of the first edition of this book.

15   Ekman, *Jean Sibelius*, 256–57.

16   Ibid., 209–210.

music is a mirror."[17] Seldom, however, does his music mirror religion as expressed in Finland's predominately Lutheran churches. With few exceptions, most of the known examples of Sibelius's organ and liturgical music appeared in the years between the establishment of the Suomi Lodge No. 1 in 1922 and the creation of "Musique réligieuse" for that lodge in 1927. In all, these works total less than a dozen short pieces, with most of them written in the same year, 1925.[18]

Although Sibelius did not compose much music specifically for liturgical use, this does not mean he divorced himself from setting texts that can be considered "religious" or "sacred" in the traditional sense of those words. Representative examples can be found throughout his career: the third (1895) and fourth (1909) songs from *Five Christmas Songs* (opus 1), which center on the light brought into the world by the birth of the Christ Child; the incidental music to Hjalmar Procopé's play, *Belshazzar's Feast* (opus 51, 1906); "Kellosävel Kallion kirkossa" ("The Bell Melody of Kallio Church") from *Two Songs* (opus 65, 1912); the incidental music to *Jedermann* (opus 83, 1916), which concludes with a joyous setting of "Gloria in excelsis Deo"; and *Joululaulu* (*Christmas Song*, 1929), written expressly for the Finnish Lutheran Evangelical Society. A recurrent theme among the texts of these works is the image of the pilgrim moving along life's pathway—a pathway that predictably leads first toward darkness and death and then toward the eternal light.

Throughout his life, Sibelius was greatly influenced by the writings of Swedish and Finnish poets and by the Finnish national epic, *Kalevala* (*The Land of the Heroes*). From these writings he drew inspiration for his music which, in turn, so sensitively and sincerely expressed Sibelius's love of his native land. Relatively few of his solo vocal works were performed outside of Scandinavian countries during his lifetime, primarily because most of them were set to Finnish or Swedish texts. His fame outside of Finland, at least until the 1930s, was therefore almost wholly dependent upon his symphonic and choral-orchestral works.

Finnish is not a Scandinavian language. It is rooted in the Fenno-Ugric family of languages and existed solely in an oral form until the sixteenth

---

17  Ibid., 233.
18  A notable late addition to Sibelius's meager corpus of organ music is *Surusoitto* (*Mourning Music*, opus 111, no. 2) composed for, and first performed at, the funeral of Axel Gallén-Kallela in Helsinki on 19 March 1931.

century when it was transformed into a written language by Mikael Agricola (c. 1510–57), the first Lutheran bishop of Turku (Åbo). Finnish, however, did not gain an equal footing with Swedish until 1863.

Prior to the nineteenth century, the Finnish people were required to use Swedish as their official language. Swedish also served as their "cultural" language, while Latin was used as their "scholarly" language.[19] Even after Russia gained supremacy over Finland in the 1808–1809 war, Swedish continued to be the dominant language. In fact, the reason that Sibelius felt more comfortable writing letters in Swedish than in Finnish was that he grew up in a home where only Swedish was spoken. It was the language of the educated minority, whereas Finnish was used almost exclusively by the uneducated majority. Although Sibelius attended the famous Hämeen Lyseo, the first lycée in Finland to conduct all instruction in the Finnish language, he never felt Finnish to be his "native" language.[20]

The person who paved the way for changing the status of the Finnish language was Elias Lönnrot (1802–84). With the publication of two literary works, he convincingly demonstrated that Finnish could indeed be a language for literature. He published *Kalevala*, the national epic, in 1835 and *Kanteletar*, a collection of lyrical folk poetry, in 1840. Lönnrot was a country doctor whose work took him into the northern regions of Finland where rune-singers kept alive, via the oral tradition, the songs and stories of the *Kalevala*. He collected and collated the various fragments of the epic, which he then published in Finnish. An initial edition appeared in 1835, followed by an expanded edition in 1849. The 1849 edition was translated into many languages and within a short time the epic became known far and wide. More than anything else it drew worldwide attention to the people, customs, and crafts of this northern country.

No less important than the poetic exaltation of beauty that pervades the whole of the *Kalevala* is the musical element. It is embodied in the figure of Väinämöinen, the old primeval minstrel who accompanies his singing of the epic's songs with the kantele, an harp-like instrument that continues to this day to be used for performing traditional Finnish folk music. With its union of music and nature, it is understandable why Sibelius was attracted to this epic as a source for several of his most important compositions. For more than one

---

19   Rossel, *A History of Scandinavian Literature 1870–1980*, 65.
20   Tawaststjerna (Layton, trans.), *Sibelius, 1865–1905*, I, 17.

hundred and fifty years, the *Kalevala* has served as the well-spring of source materials for many of Finland's artists, poets, authors, and musicians.[21]

It was only a short step from the path-breaking work of Lönnrot to the poetic emphasis on Finnish folk life and nature that one finds in the works of John Ludvig Runeberg (1804–77) and Viktor Rydberg (1828–95). In the course of his career, Sibelius wrote over one hundred songs, with more than a quarter of them set to Swedish texts by these two poets. Runeberg was a personal friend of the Sibelius family and therefore his poetry was introduced to the composer at an early age. Although Runeberg was a native of Finland, he wrote all of his poetry in Swedish. Consequently he is claimed by Sweden as one of its greatest poets of the nineteenth century. Not until the second half of that century when Alexis Kivi (1834–72) wrote his first drama, *Kullervo* (1860), and his novel, *Seitsemän veljestä* (1870), in Finnish did a true literary language develop for the people of Finland.

Runeberg is a realist. His poetry spans a wide range of styles and themes, from the patriotic narrative to the idyllic lyric. Representative of the former are his stirring verses of "Our Land," the text for Finland's national anthem. Of the latter are the poems which Sibelius used for his *Seven Songs of Runeberg* (opus 13) and *Six Songs* (opus 90).

Both Runeberg and Lönnrot are credited with awakening the Finnish people to the potential influence that native-born writers could have on the literary scene within their homeland. The significance of their contributions to this "awakening" was reaffirmed at the 1899 "Press Pension Celebrations." In the final tableau entitled "Finland Awakes," figures representing heroes of Finnish nationalism appear on stage and they include those impersonating Runeberg and Lönnrot.[22]

Rydberg, a native of Sweden, is an idealist who represents the best in Swedish literature from his generation of writers. In addition to his poems and novels, Rydberg distinguished himself as a translator (Goethe's *Faust* and Edgar Allen Poe's "The Raven") and as a researcher in the field of religious studies. Simplicity, originality, and forthrightness—these are the characteristics of his lyrical poetry. A number of Rydberg's poems were used by Sibelius for choral works such as his *Song of the Athenians* (op. 31, no.3) set for a chorus

---

21  See, for example, W. F. Kirby's translation of Elias Lönnrot's *Kalevala. The Land of Heroes*, II, 152–272 (runo xi–runo l).

22  Tawaststjerna (Layton, trans.), *Sibelius, 1865–1905*, I, 222.

of men and boys, winds, and percussion. The heroic theme found here is also present in *Snöfrid*, another Rydberg poem which Sibelius chose for a dramatic setting with narrator and male chorus. Rydberg's poetry also provided lyrics for four of the songs in Sibelius's set of *Five Songs* (op. 38), composed between 1903 and 1904.

The first two songs in this set of five, "Höstkväll" ("Autumn Evening") and "På verandan vid havet" ("On a Balcony by the Sea"), are among some of the finest that Sibelius composed and are indicative of his intense emotional response to nature. "Autumn Evening" is descriptive of nature's unfathomable power. It juxtaposes the beauty of the setting sun with the dark and foreboding clouds of an encroaching storm, and contrasts the awesomeness of nature's actions with the passiveness of the human observer who enters the final scene of the poem, an observer with whom Sibelius may have identified himself.[23] "On the Balcony" is descriptive of the ebb and flow of life's eternal quest for the Divine. A paraphrase of the question posed is, "Do you remember the awesome silence when all of life was consumed by a desire to comprehend the vastness of infinity?" Sibelius originally composed these two songs for voice and piano but later provided each with an orchestral accompaniment.

Although the poems of Runeberg and Rydberg were highly regarded by Sibelius, only Rydberg's poetry is represented among the texts used for the Masonic ritual music. His verses appear along with those of Franz von Schober, Pao Chao, Johann Wolfgang von Goethe, Augusti Simelius (Aukusti Simojoki), and Simo Korpela in the 1936 edition. When the manuscript copy of Sibelius's opus 113 arrived in New York in 1935, the score did not indicate the names or sources for the texts. Similarly, the 1936 edition failed to provide this information. Only the name of Marshall Kernochan, who created the English lyrics, was noted in the preface to the published score.

Samuli Sario and Wäinö Sola supplied verses for three additional pieces in the revised and expanded edition of the Masonic ritual music. Their names were indicated in the 1950 publication, as were those of all but one of the other authors. Although this attempt to rectify the omissions of the earlier edition was well intentioned, it unfortunately failed to fully remedy the situation because two attributions were subsequently proven to be incorrect. Texts attributed to

---

23   Ibid., I, 265.

Friedrich von Schiller and Confucius in the 1950 edition were later identified as being by Franz von Schober and Pao Chao respectively.[24]

The incorrect attributions were not the fault of the editor of the published edition. Since Sibelius believed he had indeed set the verses of Schiller and Confucius, the fault must therefore lie either with him or with the sources he was using. With the exception of a poem sent to him by Berndt Forsblom, Sibelius selected the verses that appear in his "Musique réligieuse."[25] In an undated letter written to Berndt Forsblom shortly before opus 113 was introduced to Suomi Lodge No. 1 in January 1927, Sola confirms this selection process and specifically names Schiller and Confucius among the poets whose verses Sibelius considered suitable for his ritual music.[26]

### The opus 113 texts and their authors[27]

So seldom is Franz von Schober (1798–1882) represented in collections of nineteenth-century German poetry that it is little wonder the text for the initial vocal piece (No. 2) of Sibelius's "Musique réligieuse" was not correctly attributed to him. Schober's poetry spans a wide range of styles and subjects. An unevenness in the quality of his writing is discernible, but this never deterred interest from composers who frequently chose his verses for their songs. As if to underscore the importance of having his poetry set to music, Schober indicated the name of every composer who set his verses directly below the titles of all relevant poems in his published collections.[28]

Schober was born in Sweden but spent most of his life in Austria. It was in 1815, when he was studying law in Vienna, that he first met Franz Schubert and from that time until the composer's death in 1828 they remained very close friends. More than a dozen of Schober's poems were set to music by Schubert. They include his poems about nature ("Frühlingsgesang"), love ("Cavatine"), religion ("Pax Vobiscum"), and death ("Todesmusik"). Undoubtedly his best

---

24    Marvia, *Sibeliuksen Rituaalimusiikki*, 26n1.
25    Presumably Sibelius consulted with officials of his lodge before setting these texts to music, but to date there is no information to confirm this.
26    Marvia, *Sibeliuksen Rituaalimusiikki*, 200–201. Wäinö Sola's letter has been preserved by Aimo Aine and his wife, the daughter of Berndt Forsblom, and was made available to Marvia for his research.
27    The texts are discussed in the order of their appearance in the 1950 edition.
28    See Schober, *Gedichte*, 2nd ed. (1865).

known poem is "An die Musik." It was made famous through the exceptionally fine vocal setting given it by Franz Schubert in 1817.[29]

Several of Schober's poems have as a central theme the imagery of music. In "Todesmusik" ("Death Music"), sacred music is called upon to ease the pain of one who is about to slip from an earthly to a heavenly realm. The soul becomes enveloped in harmonies and is borne on the wings of sound to be "united with the light."[30] In "Trost im Liede" ("Comfort in Song"), Schober builds upon a similar theme. When the storm of life brings misfortune, a harp is held up as a shield. It does not offer protection from the storm, but as the wind breaks each string, muted tones resonate from the instrument and bring "mysterious comfort" to a life mingled with joy and pain.[31]

As mentioned above, the lyrics in the first vocal piece of opus 113 were thought to be by Schiller. The discovery of the rightful author occurred a number of years after Sibelius's death when Aarre Heinon, a professor at Tampere University, noted a similarity between Sibelius's lyrics and "Taide," a Finnish version of Schober's "An die Musik" by Eino Leino.[32]

With the publication of more than seventy volumes of his writings, Eino Leino (1878–1926) was surely one of the more prolific Finnish writers of his generation. Although strongly influenced by the works of Goethe, Heine, and Nietzsche, his writings also bear the profound impact of a 1897 sojourn in the Karelia region of his native country. Hence, he was armed on the one hand with the ideas of pantheistic religion and universal humanism and on the other with mythology and folklore.[33] Leino also brought to the fore the theme that dominated much of the early nineteenth-century German literature to which he was particularly attracted, namely the "artist's problem." In his 1902 collection of poetry, entitled _Kangatuksia_ (_Mirages_), Leino allows his own personal struggle as an artist to find expression and justification. Through poetic imagery he lays bare the idea that not only does art demand "a total

---

29 These poems appear in the original German and in English translation in Wigmore, trans., _Schubert: The Complete Song Texts._
30 Ibid., 336.
31 Ibid., 342.
32 "Taide" ("Art") was included in an anthology of poetry published in Helsinki in 1908. See Dahlström, _Jean Sibelius._
33 Rossel, 105. Armac Eino Leopold Lönnbohn adopted Eino Leino as his pen name.

dedication of one's life," but also a "conviction that loneliness is the basis for the development of the individual."[34]

In "An die Musik," Schober personifies "art" by addressing the opening and closing lines to "Du holde Kunst" (often translated as "beloved art"). He praises her for lifting him to another world whenever he is enveloped in "life's tumultuous round." He then thanks her for revealing a "heaven of happier times."

With the exception of the title chosen for his version of Schober's poem, Leino's translation remains faithful to the original. It opens with "Suloinen taide" (literally, sweet or charming art), but these words are not found in Sibelius's score. Instead, Sibelius paraphrases Leino's poem to create lyrics that differ considerably from the original German text and the Finnish translation. For example, in Sibelius's lyrics there is no mention or allusion to music, even though Schober makes two references to it in his poem—in the title and in the second stanza that describes a harp emitting the sounds of "a celestial chord." Nor does Sibelius's opening line make any reference to art. "Suloinen taide" becomes "Suloinen aate" (charming ideas). For Sibelius and his fellow Masons, "thoughts" instead of "art" provide comfort in life's darker moments and "flames of fire," not music or art, bring light to souls in darkness.[35]

"Tedious Ways" by Pao Chao is the source from which Sibelius selected verses for No. 3 of "Musique réligieuse." It may seem strange to find fifth-century Chinese poetry represented among the verses chosen for opus 113, but this corpus of literature was quite accessible to Sibelius through various German, and even Finnish, translations. One of the highly regarded German translators of Chinese literature in the nineteenth century was Alfred Forke. His *Blüthen Chinesischer Dichtung* includes Pao Chao's poems and may have been the source used to produce the Finnish lyrics.[36]

Pao Chao (ca. 414–66) was a famous poet of the Southern Dynasties, who served in several official positions under the Liu Sung Emperor, Hsiao Wu Ti. He was secretary in the Grand Council and held various other staff positions as writer and administrator, but he could never break out of these fairly low-level roles because he was subjected to the rules of class hierarchy.[37] A rebellion

---

34   Ibid., 104.
35   Kernochan's lyrics for the 1950 edition can be viewed in Appendix II.
36   See Forke, *Blüthen Chinesischer Dichtung.*
37   Mair, ed., *The Columbia Anthology of Traditional Chinese Literature*, 492.

instigated by the Imperial Prince, Lin Tzu-hsü, whom Pao Chao also served, ultimately cost both men their lives. The Prince was forced to commit suicide and rioting soldiers assassinated Pao Chao.

Over 200 of Pao Chao's poems survive and they reveal a wide range of styles and subjects, from love poems to the traditional *fu*. His particular gift was writing ballads and poetry in the folk-song genre, with the imagery of music prevalent in many of his works.[38] For example, in his "Wu ch'eng fu" ("The Ruined City"), he describes the desolation and "awesome silence" of a city where "music and dancing" and "melodies from various states" used to flourish, and then concludes the *fu* with a song to be sung to the accompaniment of his lute.

"Tedious Ways" is a sectional work containing several untitled poems and it is from the third poem that Sibelius has drawn his verses. This poem is addressed to young people as a reminder that they should not neglect ceremonies and should maintain fellowship with friends, for they only pass through this life once. It opens with a description of autumn leaves that have fallen on the path. The poet asks, "Will they become green again?" Then follows a description of the sacrificial food laid out for the spirits, a reference no doubt to the Confucian ritual where food and wine are part of the proscribed ceremonial offerings to the divine spirit of the Great Master. The poet asks if they have noticed that the spirits have not partaken of the offerings, which is another of way of saying that humans were not present at the ceremony, for if they had been, they would have eaten the food after offering it to the spirits. The dried leaves and the uneaten food are warnings that "youthful days never return." Finally, the poet urges the youth to participate in ceremonies and to enjoy food and drink with friends as a way of dispelling worries and fear. And then, as the poet notices that his remarks have not brought pleasure to those he has addressed, he concludes with a question: "Do you not like my 'Tedious Ways'?"[39]

Eino Tikkanen's 1925 Finnish translation of this poem was used by Sibelius, and the resulting verses are very different from the Chinese original. Even further removed are the English lyrics that were created by Kernochan. In the 1936 edition, the final lines of the English lyrics read: "Better far to think of Friendship, Bound by our Fraternal Love." Although these words do not closely

---

38   Ibid., 358.
39   Three poems from "Tedious Ways" appear in English translation in Birch, ed., *Anthology of Chinese Literature form Early Times to the Fourteenth Century*, 189–90.

adhere to Tikkanen's Finnish words, they at least carry forth the spirit of the original Chinese. For the 1950 edition, Kernochan once again changed the final lines: "Let him trust his heart for guidance! Where, O Death, is then thy sting?" It is difficult to imagine anything more incongruous with the original Chinese, yet these words are entirely appropriate for the Master Mason ritual. The initiate is reminded that "nature presents one great and useful lesson," namely knowledge of oneself:

> She leads you by contemplation to the closing hours of your existence…. She leads you to reflect upon your inevitable destiny, and prompts the inward monitor to say that death has no sting equal to the stain of falsehood, and that the certainty of death at any time is better than the possibility of dishonor.[40]

No. 4 of "Musique réligieuse" is subdivided into three sections, with the first two for the organ alone and the third, a hymn, for voice and organ. The text for the hymn comes from Johann Wolfgang von Goethe's "Harfenspieler: II" ("The Harper's Songs: II"), one of four poems that appear in book four of his theatrical novel *Wilhelm Meister* (1783). It is introduced by the Harpist, an elderly man with a white beard and blue eyes, draped in a long black robe. He is a wandering minstrel, reminiscent of Väinämöinem in the *Kalevala*, and represents one who stands apart from society. The Harpist sings to Wilhelm and his itinerant theatrical group, as they prepare to go to another city looking for work, and his song opens with the line "Wie nie sein Brot mit Tränen ass" ("He who has never eaten his bread with tears").[41]

By the time Goethe was born in Frankfurt am Main in 1749, Freemasonry had already been introduced into his city. Calvinist merchants established the first Masonic lodge there in 1742. So rapid was the introduction of Freemasonry on German soil from the 1740s onward that by the 1770s a majority of the German intellectuals had become members of the Craft. As Masonry grew, so too did secret societies throughout continental Europe. It is therefore understandable why aspects of fraternal life frequently are mentioned in literature of the period, as, for example, in the writings of Lessing.

---

40   *Monitor of the Work, Lectures and Ceremonies of Ancient Craft Masonry*, 62.
41   Boyle, *Goethe, the Poet and the Age*, I, 369.

In 1782, just two years after Goethe became a Mason, he declared that he was neither anti-Christian nor un-Christian, but simply non-Christian.[42] Goethe adopted this posture after becoming convinced that God had fully revealed himself in "nature" and therefore the Bible and the organized church were of little importance to him. Although he held respect for the Christian church, he did not attend services of worship.

Goethe's writings often reflect his deep knowledge about Freemasonry. This is especially evident in *The Mysteries*, an incomplete epic poem of nearly fifty stanzas written between 1784 and 1785. It was also in the mid-1780s that German Freemasonry was undergoing a difficult period. There were two schools of thought about its purpose and goals: the Rosicrucians thought emphasis should be on mythology and rituals while the Illuminists thought it should be on philosophical and ethical issues. Before the matter could be debated at length within the Craft, the Bavarian government accused the Illuminists of fostering a republican conspiracy and decreed that new members could not be recruited to Masonry. The effects of the decree lasted for some twenty years, during which time many lodges were forced to close. Goethe needed little more than this controversy to convince him that his days as a faithful member of his lodge would be numbered. His disillusionment with the practices of Freemasonry is parodied in his 1790 Masonic comedy, "Das Gross-Cophta" ("The Grand Kophta"), wherein the principal character becomes a Mason because he believed the brotherhood was dedicated to "missionary altruism."[43] Only later, after his initiation, did he find out that this was not true.

"Harfenspieler: II" consists of two stanzas and in this form was first set to music by Schubert in 1816. When it was set by Sibelius, only the first stanza was used. Unlike the poems by Schober and Pao Chao which bear but a faint resemblance to the lyrics that finally appeared in opus 113, Goethe's poem received a very literal translation in both Finnish and English. Was this because Sibelius was already well acquainted with the writings of Goethe in their original language or was it because recent translations of Goethe's works into Finnish had made the poems accessible to a wider audience in Finland?[44]

---

42    Ibid., 363.
43    Ibid., 274.
44    Sibelius used a Finnish translation of Goethe's poem by Eino Leino, published in Helsinki in 1913. See Dahlström, *Jean Sibelius*. By the 1920s there were available to Sibelius a number of other Finnish translations of Goethe's works, such as those of Otto Manninen (1872–1950), from which he could have drawn his text.

Kernochan's lyrics for the 1936 edition closely parallel both the original German and Finnish translations:

Who ne'er has tasted Sorrow's bread,
Comfortless vigils, nights of anguish;
Specters that mock all hope of solace,
He shall not see the Light of Heaven.

For the 1950 edition, he revised these lyrics, creating an even more effective paraphrase of Goethe's original text.[45]

Of all the texts in the 1927 version of opus 113, the one that most expresses the joyful spirit of nature is "How fair are Earth and Living!" ("On kaunis maa"), which was set as No. 5 of "Musique réligieuse." It is by Augustus Simelius (1882–1959), a professor well known in Finland for his sensitive translations of poetry.[46] As was noted in an earlier chapter, Berndt Forsblom sent this text to Sibelius and suggested he might create a musical setting for it. His suggestion was rewarded by Sibelius's delicate, dream-like interpretation of the poem.[47] Kernochan's lyrics follow fairly closely the Finnish text, which declaims the beauty of the night sky and the awesomeness of the celestial spheres. Through this imagery, the poet urges mankind to seek thoughts as lofty as the heavens so that peace and hope may fill the days of one's life.

Two of the numbers in opus 113 have lyrics based on "Cantata," a poem by Rydberg that was written for the graduation festivities at Upsala University on 6 September 1877, an event that also marked the 400th anniversary of that institution.[48] Rydberg's poem opens with a structure similar to that of a church cantata: a substantial introductory chorus, a recitative and *arioso*, and a brief concluding chorus that repeats the final lines of the *arioso*. This whole "cantata" section functions as a prologue, its message directed to all of the graduates. The poem then continues with four separate sections, each of equal length (eight lines of free verse), which are directed to the graduates within specific disciplines of the university curriculum—Theology, Jurisprudence, Medicine,

---

45   For the 1950 version, see Appendix II, no. 5, item no. 4.
46   After 1935, he preferred to be known as Aukusti Simojoki.
47   According to Marvia, in *Sibeliuksen Rituaalimusiikki*, 30, the original title given to this hymn was "Valo" ("Light"), suggesting an intended placement within the Masonic ritual.
48   It has been common practice in Finland, even up to the present day, to have well-known composers write cantatas for performance at university graduation ceremonies.

and Philosophy. Sibelius used the words from the *arioso* for No. 7 of his ritual music, "Who so ever hath a love of justice" ("Kella kaipuu rinnassansa"), and the words from the "Philosphy" portion of the Rydberg's poem for No. 6, "Onward, ye Brethren" ("Kulje, kansa, kohti määrä).

The opening section of Rydberg's "Cantata" admonishes the graduate to strive toward "the good" along life's uncharted path. Even though one's existence within the earthly realm is but a fleeting moment, one can outlast time and space with "noble thoughts, acts of love, and dreams of beauty," for they will be impregnated in the hearts and minds of future generations. Rydberg draws together the essence of the entire prologue in the *arioso*. Here he emphasizes that trust in the Divine will allow each person to achieve immortality, just as those of past generations have been brought to the river Jordan.

All four of the "discipline" sections of Rydberg's "Cantata" are related to particular passages in the Bible. That for the "Philosophy" section is related to Exodus 13:21 and Deuteronomy 34. The passage from Exodus describes how God led Israel out of Egypt: "the Lord went before them by day in a pillar of cloud to lead them and by night in a pillar of fire to give them light, that they may travel by day and night." Deuteronomy 34 relates how Moses went up from the plains of Moab to Mount Nebo and was shown the land which God promised to give to his descendants. Rydberg freely paraphrases the ideas expressed in the biblical passages and once again he urges the graduates to strive towards "the goal God hath placed" before them. The path to that goal may be difficult to discern, but the way will be illuminated by pillars of cloud and fire. As a final word of assurance, the path-seeker will hear the voice of one shouting from Nebo, "Forward to the land ye seek!"[49]

Sibelius set Rydberg's original Swedish texts, but then had them translated into Finnish by Samuli Sario before the first complete performance of opus 113 took place in January of 1927.[50] Both versions, however, were kept in the score with the Finnish placed under the Swedish lyrics. The dual texts also were retained in the 1935 manuscript presented to the GLNY and in the Funtek orchestral score.[51]

---

49   Stork, trans., *Anthology of Swedish Lyrics from 1750 to 1925*, 118–24.

50   The Swedish text in No. 6 is not identical to Rydberg's original poem. Sibelius changed Rydberg's "när han är" to "när hon är" and "Fram till…fram!" to "Fram mot…fram!"

51   Kernochan's lyrics for these two Rydberg texts sometimes give but a faint glimmer of the structure or sense of either the Swedish or Finnish lyrics. For example, in "Onward, ye Brethren!" ("Kulje, kansa, kohti määrä") two lines of the text are repeated in both the

In addition to the eight selections originally included in what Sibelius titled "Musique réligieuse," the 1935 manuscript (MS-113-35) contained Sibelius's chorale setting of Jacob Tegengren's "Den höga himlen," which by the late 1920s had also become incorporated into ritual use at SSL. Tegengren's text, a Swedish translation of Simo Korpela's "Suur' olet, Herra," is afforded a fairly literal translation in the 1936 edition. The chorale text is a hymn of praise to the "Architect Supreme," sung by all creation, in heaven and on earth. It expresses awe and adoration of the power of the Divine Word by which even the planets are caused to move: "Before Thy Holy Name we bow the knee."

Between 1935 and 1948, when the revised and expanded manuscript (MS-113-48) of opus 113 was sent to the GLNY and Galaxy, Sibelius contributed several more selections to the corpus of ritual music for use by Suomi Lodge No. 1 and SSL. Two of these had texts especially created for this purpose by Samuli Sario, an active member of Freemasonry in Helsinki since the 1920s. As has already been discussed, it was this same Sario who had been called upon to transformed Rydberg's Swedish lyrics into Finnish so that the first complete performance of opus 113 in January 1927 could be sung throughout in the Finnish language.

Unlike the other texts mentioned above, Sario's texts speak directly to Masonic ideals. "Ode to Fraternity" ("Veljesvirsi") is addressed to the "Brethren" and focuses on the fraternal bond of unity. The opening phrase of the first verse is repeated as a refrain: "Good and pleasant 'tis for Brethren to dwell in unity." The second verse touches upon the right actions of Masons, not only in their personal lives but also in their relationships to those in society who need "a helping hand." The text for "Hymn" ("Ylistyshymni") echoes the sentiments expressed in the Tegengren/Korpela text, namely, it is an expression of praise to the "Architect Supreme" and an affirmation of faith in the "Father Omnipotent." As a way of reinforcing this "credo," the English lyrics incorporate phrases from the Nicene Creed: "O God of God, O Light of Light, O Very God of Very God."

Also included with the 1948 manuscript was the Sibelius-Sola "Finlandia-Hymni." In Finnish lodges, "Finlandia-Hymni" does not form an official part of the ritual music used for degree work, but its inclusion in the manuscript and in the 1950 edition placed it in a different category for the Masons in

---

original Swedish and the Finnish translations, but they are not repeated in the English version.

New York. Wäinö Sola's text is not specifically "Masonic" and therefore is not restricted to Masonic activities. The first verse asks God to bless "our native land," and to keep it free from "war's relentless hand." The second verse affirms peoples' reliance on "Thy wisdom" and their thanksgiving for "the precious gifts from Thee."[52]

In contrast to Sola's lyrics, those supplied by Marshall Kernochan for the 1950 edition are addressed to the fraternity and therefore are considered "Masonic." The last two lines of the first verse read:

> To Thee our Brothers pray for truth and justice
> And in Thy faith they firmly take their stand.

When the "Finlandia Hymn" was issued as a separate non-Masonic publication by Galaxy, Kernochan changed several words and phrases, including the last two lines:

> To Thee our peoples pray for truth and justice
> And in Thy faith united they stand.

In order for Kernochan to create English lyrics for the printed editions of opus 113, he had to find someone who could provide him with English translations of the Finnish texts. The person he turned to for the first edition was George (Yrjö) Sjöblom, a resident of Brooklyn with whom Kernochan was well acquainted. When Kernochan started work on the second edition of opus 113, he did not involve Sjöblom in translating the three new items or in revising the translations for items previously published in 1936. Either Kernochan did not ask Sjöblom, or if he did, Sjöblom declined. This seems a bit odd, given the fact that Sjöblom and Sibelius had known each other ever since 1915 and, even more importantly (although Kernochan did not know this at the time), that Sjöblom was the first person to create a text in Finnish for the "Finlandia-Hymni," one of the three new items requiring translation.

For reasons known only to Kernochan, he had Toivo Nekton produce new translations for the texts of all the vocal numbers that were to appear in the 1950 edition.[53] The choice of Nekton was possibly predicated upon several

---

52   For a discussion of the "Finlandia Hymn," see chapter seven.
53   As was explained in a previous chapter, Sola provided Nekton with a manuscript (MS-113-48tn) that included the Finnish texts.

factors: the close friendship he and Wäinö Sola had had for many years; the ongoing correspondence which Nekton and Sola had about the revised edition; and the experience and knowledge of the Masonic ritual that Nekton had so convincingly demonstrated in 1922.[54] After Nekton completed his task, Kernochan wrote English lyrics for the three new items and also revised the lyrics he had previously supplied for the 1936 edition.

---

54  More than twenty letters were exchanged between Toivo Nekton and Wäinö Sola in the period extending from April 1948 to January 1950. For a list of their letters in the SSL archives, see Marvia, *Sibeliuksen Rituaalimusiikki*, 210–11.

# CHAPTER SEVEN

## THE "FINLANDIA HYMN"

The hymn "Finlandia," arranged from the orchestral work that bears the same title, is well-known throughout the world. What is not so well known is how Sibelius's own version of this hymn for male chorus came to be created. Ever since the music was first heard in connection with the "Press Pension Celebrations" in 1899, the patriotic spirit associated with that initial performance has lived on in other performances. Although many and various poetic verses have been wed to the "Finlandia" hymn, only the verses by Wäinö Sola (in Finnish) and by Marshall Kernochan (in English) have been used by the Masons in conjunction with their lodge activities.

In February of 1899, Czar Nicholas II issued a manifesto that severely curtailed the legislative powers vested in the Finnish Parliament. This unexpected action from the pen of the Russian ruler sparked a wave of protests among the intellectuals in Finland. Sibelius was infuriated by the manifesto and vented his protest in the *Song of the Athenians* (*Atenarnes sång*, opus 31) set for a men and boys chorus, wind septet, and percussion. It was performed for the first time 26 April 1899 as the concluding work for a concert of Sibelius's music and greatly stirred the nationalistic passions of those in the audience.[1]

This was not the first, nor the last, of Sibelius's "protest" compositions. A year earlier, in 1898, he had composed *The Breaking of the Ice on the River Ulea* (*Islossningen i Uleå älv*, opus 30). Scored for male chorus (TTBB), narrator, and orchestra, the text speaks of freedom and national pride:

---

1    Tawaststjerna (Layton, trans.), I, 208.

Whose slave am I in my pride of youth
Needs stand in bond through endless winter?
Noble son of Finland's blue lakes
I was born free and free I will die.[2]

By the autumn of 1899, Czarist threats to curtail freedom of expression in the press were mounting and the Finnish people looked for ways to demonstrate their support for those disseminating the news. On 4 November 1899, an event known as the "Press Pension Celebrations" was held on the pretext of raising funds for the pensions of those associated with the press in Finland. It was, in fact, an event designed specifically to raise the public's awareness of its national heritage. The highlight of the "Celebrations" was the staging of six historical tableaux, with texts by Jalmari Finne and Eino Leino and orchestral music by Sibelius. Following the playing of the overture, each of the six tableaux was introduced by a separate instrumental piece and then accompanied by muted orchestral music during the spoken commentary on the event being portrayed. In all, Sibelius composed seven separate instrumental pieces. The last of them, the "Finale," introduced the tableau entitled "Finland Awakes."

Soon after the staging of the tableaux in the Swedish Theater, Sibelius was asked by Axel Carpelan to write an overture for the concert that would open the Paris World Exhibition. Carpelan, in an anonymous note to the composer, suggested the overture be called "Finlandia" in order to place before the international audience the name of their homeland. Sibelius did not bother to compose a new work for the Exhibition. He simply removed the "Finale" title and replaced it with "Finlandia."[3]

The "Press Pension Celebrations" score was never given an opus number. Only when Sibelius revised and regrouped individual items from it were they assigned their own opus numbers. On 14 December 1899, Robert Kajanus conducted a concert in Helsinki that included four instrumental sections of the "Press" score. They were performed as a group under the title "Kuvaelmanmusiikkia." Three of the four pieces were assigned to opus 25. The fourth, the "Finale," became opus 26.[4] A year later the "Finale" was again revised and became what

---

2    Ibid., I, 219.
3    Ibid., I, 222.
4    Dahlström, *The Works of Jean Sibelius*, 72.

is now known as the tone poem *Finlandia* (opus 26, no. 7), the no. 7 denoting its original position in the "Press" score.

When the Czar of Russia realized how effectively "Finlandia" had stirred the patriotic emotions of the Finnish people, he moved quickly to ban the music, declaring any performance of it "inside the realm" would constitute "an act of treason."[5] Reaction to the Czar's decree was predictable. What was forbidden became intensely desired.

From its first performance in Helsinki on 2 July 1900 to the present, the tone poem *Finlandia* has been extremely popular, not only as an orchestral work but also in arrangements for solo piano or symphonic band, among other instrumental variants. Equally popular is the hymn-like tune which was lifted out from the middle section of the tone poem. People around the world found themselves attracted to this portion of the score and adapted their own lyrics to the music. Nowhere was this music from *Finlandia* more readily available than in the various hymnbooks published in the United States and distributed worldwide.

Although lyrics for the "Finlandia" hymn have been written in many different languages, it is believed that the first set of lyrics in the Finnish language, "written and sung widely ... over a long stretch of time," was created by George (Yrjö) Sjöblom in 1919.[6] George Sjöblom was born in Finland in 1889 and brought to the United States as an infant by his parents. He developed into a person of many talents, but it was his talent as a writer and editor that encouraged him to devote his life to the newspaper business. After working for several Finnish-American papers, he joined the staff of *The New York Times* and held his position there until he retired in 1966.[7]

In addition to his work for the *Times*, Sjöblom was actively engaged in writing articles about Finland and by organizing concert tours in America for Finnish

---

5    Paul Sjöblom, "An Interview with Sibelius," *Musical America* 50 (10 Dec 1940):11, 34. The tone-poem was also performed under the title "Impromptu" to hide its patriotic and nationalistic origins.

6    Paul Sjöblom, "Finlandia as a Song and the Contribution of George Sjöblom," *Finnish American Horizons* (1976):259-60. This article is based on an article, in Finnish, by his father. See Yrjö [George] Sjöblom, "Finlandia Lauluna," *Suomen Kiivalehti* no. 49 (8 Dec 1949):1258-59.

7    Obituary for George Sjöblom, *The New York Times* (4 Aug 1971):36. According to his son, Paul, George Sjöblom continued to be associated with the *Times* on a part-time basis from 1966 until 1970, one year before his death. For more on George Sjöblom as a writer, see chapter four.

musicians. Sjöblom was also active as an amateur musician, participating in brass bands and Finnish-American choral groups. Not the least of his activities was the founding in 1915 of the Sibelius Club in Monessen (PA) for the purpose of fostering Finnish music (in print and in performance) in America.[8]

It was in 1919 that Sjöblom was inspired to write lyrics for the "hymn" section of *Finlandia*.[9] He was away from home on assignment in Calumet, Michigan, and was feeling particularly lonesome one Sunday in December when a snowstorm kept him confined to his rented room. As he gazed out the window, watching the storm, he recalled a description of *Finlandia* that he had recently read in Erik Furuhjelm's monograph on Sibelius, published in 1916. After describing the sound and fury of the opening section of the tone poem, Furuhjelm turns to the "hymn" section and writes:

> Silence prevails, then a new melody is heard—a marvelously simple and pure melody, extraordinarily profound in content, powerfully stirring in its ethical nobility. It is a hymn for the masses.... Never has a son of Finland created anything more patriotically uplifting than this magnificent tone poem, *Finlandia*.[10]

Sjöblom found himself humming the hymn tune and little by little words began to form themselves into rhymed couplets and then into verses. A few months later when Sjöblom rejoined his family in Warren, Ohio, he revised his poem and set the lyrics to Herbert S. Sammond's choral arrangement of the hymn section of *Finlandia*. Sjöblom's verses appear to be the only ones in Finnish that were shared publicly until 1936 when Martti Nisonen, a Finnish musician who had immigrated to the United States, came forth with his verses in both Finnish and English.[11]

---

8    In a letter (17 Jan 1964) to Rev. R. N. Foltz of Monessen (PA), George Sjöblom chronicles his life in this Pennsylvania community from 1915 to 1919. It was during this period, as secretary of the Sibelius Club, that his earliest correspondence with Sibelius began. For example, he had to ask Sibelius for permission to use his name for the newly formed club. He also had to make arrangements for the Louhi Band of Finnish musicians to visit the composer in Finland in 1919. Although Sjöblom was a member of the band, he was unable to take this trip because that same year he accepted a position as editor-in-chief for *Valvoja* in Calumet, Michigan. This letter is in SFC.

9    Yrjö [George] Sjöblom, "Finlandia lauluna," *Suomen Kuvalehti* (8 Dec 1945):49.

10   Paul Sjöblom, "Finlandia as a Song," 262.

11   Ibid., 260, 263.

Not before 1937 did someone living in Finland create verses in Finnish intended for public use with the "Finlandia" hymn and that person was Wäinö Sola. One reason why the Finnish people may not have shown much interest in writing verses for the hymn before this date is that the "Finlandia" hymn was not being sung throughout Finland the way it was, and has continued to be, in the United States.[12]

Ever since his first hearing of the tone poem *Finlandia* in 1902, Wäinö Sola was inspired by the music. According to Einari Marvia, Sola found that "the Finlandia composition, in its entirety, is like a prediction of the future for awakening Finland. It is like an illustrated story of our nation's love of freedom and longing and desire for independence."[13] It was this spirit of patriotism that stirred the creative muse within Sola. Three decades later when he offered his verses for the "Finlandia-Hymni," he did so in the hope that the music would someday become a new national anthem for his country, replacing the rather unpopular "Maamme laulu" by Runeberg and Pacius. He even envisioned the hymn being used in connection with Masonic activities.

On 4 February 1937, Sola sent a letter to Sibelius and enclosed the verses he had written for the hymn. He kept the name of the author a secret because he wanted Sibelius to provide a fair and impartial opinion about the effectiveness of the lyrics for the musical setting. Much to his surprise, Sibelius not only liked the verses but even offered to prepare an arrangement of the hymn for male chorus. After Sola made some revisions to the text, Sibelius completed his arrangement for a TTBB chorus in 4 April 1938, just in time for its first performance at the tenth anniversary celebration of the founding of the St. John's Lodge No. 4 in Helsinki, where Sola was a member. The performance was given on 21 April 1938 by a male quartet (Wäinö Sola, Martti Similä, Sulo Räikkönen, and O. A. Turunen) accompanied by Arvi Karvonen playing the harmonium *colla parte*.[14] The first public performance of this same arrangement

---

12  Sjöblom's Finnish lyrics for "Finlandia" were sung quite frequently in the United States by Finnish choral groups. For example, the New Yorkin Laulajat (conducted by Jallu Honkonen) sang his lyrics in a concert presented on 28 October 1934 at the Evangelical Lutheran Church in Worcester (MA). The program is in SFC.

13  [Einari Marvia], "The Ritual Music of Jean Sibelius" [typescript], 9.

14  There are two manuscripts of this TTBB arrangement, both in Wäinö Sola's hand. One manuscript contains corrections in Sibelius's hand. Note that the date "4/4/37" appears at the top of one of these manuscripts and directly above that date is written "H:ki 4/4/38." These manuscript materials are in the Sibelius Museum archives (UBHels 1819). See also Marvia, *Sibeliuksen Rituaalimusiikki*, 170 and Dahlström, *Jean Sibelius*.

was heard on the occasion of a church concert in Pori on 26 December 1938. This time the choral parts were sung by a men's chorus.

In the summer of 1938, George Sjöblom and his wife traveled to Finland and visited Wäinö Sola at his home. In the course of their conversation, Sola told how he had been inspired "the summer before" to write verses to be sung to the *Finlandia* hymn tune and that Sibelius had recently arranged the music for a male *a cappella* chorus to go with his text. Sjöblom asked to see Sola's text, but when he looked at the verses, he could scarcely believe what he read. Sola's verses were incredibly similar to those he had composed in 1919.[15]

During that same trip, Sjöblom visited Sibelius and told him how popular his "Finlandia" hymn had become in the United States. In response to his guest's information, Sibelius said: "What can be done about it? It was not intended to be sung. It was written for the orchestra. But, if the world wants to sing it, there's nothing we can do about it."[16]

Personal friends of Sibelius were not the only ones welcomed to Ainola in the late 1930s. In July of 1939 members of the Yale Glee Club traveled to Helsinki to present a series of concerts. Their mission was to reinforce, through their performances, the friendship existing between the United States and Finland. One of the highlights of their visit was an invitation for all sixty members of the chorus to meet Sibelius at his country home.[17]

By the end of the 1930s, Finland was opening itself to the world. It abandoned its narrowly defined nationalistic stance and sought to embrace the ideas of other nations, especially those of France, England, and the United States. Finland was attracting particular attention at the New York World's Fair where its moment in glory no longer was inextricably dependent upon the fame of its illustrious composer.

It was also at the end of the 1930s when Russia started to worry about defending its border cities and gaining access to various sea ports to strengthen its fortifications against hostile foes. In 1938 Russia began holding secret negotiations with Finland about a possible exchange of territory to achieve these goals. Of particular interest was an area of land west of Leningrad (St. Petersburg). A year later, when these negotiations failed to produce the desired results, Russia made public its threats to take the territory from Finland by

---

15    Paul Sjöblom, "Finlandia as a Song," 263.
16    Ibid., 265.
17    "Yale Glee Singers Visit Sibelius in Helsingfors," *The New York Times* (9 July 1939):21.

force. Finland did not take these threats seriously because the possibility of a territorial war with Russia seemed remote at best.

It was therefore quite a shock to the Finnish people to find themselves invaded by the Russians in November 1939. Thus began the brief but costly Russo-Finnish Winter War, which inflicted untold casualties on the people of both countries. Some of Sibelius's closest friends suffered personal tragedies. Among them was Wäinö Sola, whose son, Pentti, was killed in that war.[18] Another was Axel Solitander, who was severely wounded when the Russians bombed Helsinki at the beginning of December 1939.[19] It was Solitander, the former Finnish Consul General in New York from 1919 to 1922 and the Grand Master of SSL, who had personally delivered Sibelius's gift of the "Musique réligieuse" to the GLNY in 1935.

Several prominent intellectuals died in that first December bombing raid over Helsinki. Among those reported killed was Sibelius and news of his apparent death spread quickly. In an effort to help dispel this false report, *The New York Times* printed two articles about the incident. The first brief article on 2 December made clear that Sibelius was not dead.[20] The second article on 3 December not only carried Sibelius's personal remarks to the American people about the incident but also included a good-sized photo of him smoking his cigar. This was done, no doubt, on the premise that "a picture is worth a thousand words."[21]

The mere thought of Sibelius being killed in the Winter War bolted New Yorkers into action. Messages of support for the Finnish nation and fund-raising events to provide monetary relief were front page news. On behalf of his country, Sibelius expressed his gratitude to Americans for their expressions of concern for the Finnish people, fostered through their awareness and appreciation of his music.[22]

The harshest winter conditions imaginable prevailed in the north of Finland as the Finnish army set out to repel the Russian army's advances. That the army accomplished its mission was nothing short of a miracle. Against all odds and in the midst of a blizzard with temperatures more than thirty degrees below

---

18   Communication from Einari Marvia to the author (13 Oct 1995).
19   "Sibelius's Death Denied," *The New York Times* (2 Dec 1939):3.
20   Ibid.
21   "Sibelius Is Safe At Finnish Forest Home," *The New York Times* (3 Dec 1939):52.
22   "Sibelius Sends Message," *The New York Times* (20 Dec 1939):5.

zero, the Finnish army was able to turn the tide of the war. As one reporter noted, "General Winter" had come to the aid of the Finns.[23]

During the last week of December in 1939, a benefit concert for the Finnish people was held at Carnegie Hall. Performing were the NBC Orchestra, conducted by Eugene Goossens, along with Scandinavian and American artists. Among the works heard that evening were *Finlandia* and *En Saga* by Sibelius. The week before the concert took place, *The New York Times* carried an article by Olin Downes in which he reminded his readers why this music was uniquely reflective of the Finnish people and their quest for liberty, for they were composed when Finland was fighting for freedom and justice.[24]

The Winter War ended in March of 1940 with the signing of an armistice. Stories of Finnish patriotism and heroism once again inspired poetical treatment of the "Finlandia" hymn. This time it was V. A. Koskenniemi (1885–1962), one of Finland's celebrated poets, who took his turn in writing verses. Koskenniemi was asked by both the director (Martii Turunen) and president (Toivo Aro) of Laulu-Miehet, a men's chorus, to create a text to sing with Sibelius's TTBB arrangement of the "Finlandia-Hymni." Koshenniemi completed the poem in the summer of 1940 and subsequently had it published in a collection of his poetry under the title "Latuja lumessa" ("Tracks in the Snow").[25] The poem was dedicated to the wounded and disabled of the Winter War (1939–40).

Before Koskenniemi's poem could be sung to the "Finlandia" tune, some minor revisions had to be made. The lyrics were ready in September of 1940, as indicated in a letter to Sibelius, and the first performance of the Koskenniemi version for male chorus (TTBB) was given by Laulu-Miehet on 7 December 1940 in Helsinki. The occasion was the 25th anniversary celebration of this vocal organization.[26]

Koskenniemi's text was also set to a mixed chorus version of "Finlandia" in 1940. Numerous publications of both these choral versions were issued between

---

23  "News of the Week in Review," *The New York Times* (24 Dec 1939):IV,1.

24  Downes, "A Composer and His Nation," *The New York Times* (20 Dec 1939):IX, 7. For an excerpt quoted from this article see page 88 of the first edition of this book.

25  Dahlström, *Jean Sibelius*. See the section on "Finlandia."

26  The Laulu-Miehet chorus also sang the Sibelius-Koskenniemi version of "Finlandia" at a concert given May 1941 in New York City's Town Hall. Kramer heard this performance and immediately wrote to Sibelius to ask if Galaxy might publish this particular arrangement with the Finnish text and an English translation of the same by George Sjöblom. See letter from A. Walter Kramer to Sibelius (21 May 1941) in the "Sibelius Family Collection 36/94," National Archives of Finland.

1940 and 1965. Some had Koskenniemi's original Finnish lyrics; others had translations of his text in Swedish (by Joel Rundts), in German (by Hellmuth von Hase), and in English (by Aina Swan Cuttler).[27]

When Sjöblom had an opportunity to see the Koskenniemi version of "Finlandia," he was astonished that this 1940 set of verses in Finnish was again very similar to his own. It was then that Sjöblom decided he could no longer refrain from letting the people of Finland know that he was the first to write lyrics in Finnish for Sibelius's music. In 1945 a Finnish journal published his description of how he came to write his "Finlandia" lyrics in 1919. In the article, Sjöblom discusses the lyrics created by Sola and Koskenniemi and shows how similar they are to his. For example, he mentions that each of the three poems speaks about pushing back the dark shadows of night to allow the dawning of a new day. Each draws upon a similar vocabulary to suggest that out of the darkness of war there can arise good fortune, out of the sufferings can come hope, peace, and prosperity.[28]

George Sjöblom did not use the article to accuse Sola or Koskenniemi of plagiarism. He graciously tried to account for the similarities in the three texts by claiming the music must have stirred similar emotions in the three authors. Privately, however, he told his son Paul that he was convinced Sola had heard or seen his verses in the 1920s and 1930s during his concert tours in the United States. Paul Sjöblom revealed his father's private thoughts in an article published in 1976.[29]

Interestingly, George Sjöblom was not alone in his opinion that the Finnish verses he wrote for the "Finlandia" hymn were the inspiration for those penned by Sola and Koskenniemi. Einari Marvia came to the same conclusion. He analyzed all three poems and found that those by Sola and Koskenniemi were indeed very similar to, even dependent upon, the 1919 poem. In the case of the opening stanza, Marvia noted that Koskenniemi actually repeated "almost word for word two pairs of verses of Sjöblom's poem."[30]

Prior to 1945, the Sjöblom version of "Finlandia" was sung by Finnish-American choruses in the greater New York City region. After 1945 it was the Koskenniemi version that was sung. This change occurred when Jussi Himanka,

---

27   Ibid.
28   Yrjö [George] Sjöblom, "Finlandia lauluna," 1259.
29   Paul Sjöblom, "Finlandia as a Song," 264.
30   Ibid. See also Marvia, *Sibeliuksen Rituaalimusiikki*, 170–72.

an immigrant to the United States at the end of World War II, became the new conductor of the Finnish Male Singers of New York. Since the only version of the "Finlandia" hymn he had known in Finland was the one by Koskenniemi, he decided to substitute it for the Sjöblom version. He did this even though George Sjöblom was still a member of the chorus and had served as president of the Finnish Male Singers since its founding.[31]

Although the "Finlandia-Hymni" was not used for any ritual function for the lodges in Finland, it nevertheless was often sung by lodge members at the conclusion of their meetings during the time of fellowship. Books containing songs suitable for this purpose were available in most lodges in Finland and the United States. Since the texts of songs used for social comradery did not have to be associated with anything that was Masonic, the pool from which they could be drawn was endless. The text Sola set to Sibelius's TTBB arrangement of the hymn fell into this category. It was not specifically Masonic and this meant his version could be performed by Masons and non-Masons alike. It should be noted, however, that it was Sola's, and not Koskenniemi's, version that was usually sung by the Masons in Finland.[32]

For many the "Finlandia" hymn had become, and continues to be, a "hymn of liberty." Leopold Stokowski, after conducting a 1940 performance of the orchestral tone poem *Finlandia*, was moved to say to the audience: "When some day in a happier future, a common 'national anthem' is written for all the nations of the earth, then the music for it should be *Finlandia*."[33] Sola, who had dreamed of making "Finlandia" a national anthem, must have been heartened to learn that Stokowksi had also envisioned this hymn becoming the world's "anthem," so powerful was its image of freedom.

Stokowski's admiration for *Finlandia* spanned several decades. It began with the 1914–1915 concert season when, as conductor of the Philadelphia Orchestra, he was the first to introduce this tone poem to audiences in that city. What particularly intrigued Stokowski was the patriotic scenario that first brought the *Finlandia* score to light and that is why he often placed this work

31   Paul Sjöblom, "Finlandia as a Song," 265.
32   See, for example, the Finnish edition of Sibelius's *Masonic Ritual Music* published in 1969.
33   Paul Sjöblom includes these remarks by Stokowski in "Finlandia As Song," 258, citing his source as follows: "Retranslated from a Finnish report, which mentions 1940 as the date when the statement was made." Stokowski's remarks are also quoted in Finnish by George Sjöblom at the beginning of his article on "Finlandia." See Yjrö [George] Sjöblom, "Finlandia lauluna," 1258.

on programs with a similar intent. For example, when he lead the New Jersey WPA Philharmonic Orchestra in a concert given for soldiers stationed at Fort Dix, he purposely included *Finlandia* on that program.[34]

How strongly associated with the nation of Finland this single musical composition had become in the 1940s is revealed in a letter published on the editorial page of *The New York Times* in October of 1942. The writer strongly advised that "Finlandia," which seemed to function as a national anthem, should not be played while Finland was allied with Germany in fighting Allied forces. The writer, however, went out of her way to emphasize that the proposed ban on "Finlandia" for the duration of the armed conflict in no way implied a ban on other compositions by Sibelius.[35]

Following the Winter War, Finland tried to remain neutral and independent during World War II, but this proved impossible for such a tiny country. In order to protect itself from Russia, Finland increasingly became aligned with Germany and it was this appearance of sympathy with the Nazis that provoked Americans to speak out against the Finnish people. As early as 1940, Sibelius pleaded with Americans for understanding of his nation's actions, and he continued to raise his voice in the press as a way of keeping alive the friendship that had grown between the two countries.

Although Sibelius's family and his home remained secure for the duration of World War II, the composer was not immune from the ravages of that conflict. Financial woes had always been a part of the composer's life, but during the war he suffered a considerable loss of revenue, not the least of which was non-payment of royalties from his American contracts. How some of these financial problems were resolved following the end of the war is discussed in a later chapter.

Sibelius included his TTBB *a cappella* arrangement of "Finlandia" as an integral part of the 1948 manuscript of his Masonic ritual music, which Sola had prepared for the revised and expanded edition published by the GLNY. Although Marshall Kernochan had access to a translation of the Finnish lyrics by Sola, he did not feel bound by them when creating his own lyrics. He decided that the whole of the second edition should be treated as a Masonic work and

---

34   See Daniel, *Stokowski, A Counterpoint of View* (New York: Dodd, Mead, 1982), 149, 331. See also "Stokowski Leads at Dix," *The New York Times* (20 Oct 1942):20.

35   Gold, "Would Ban 'Finlandia' Now," *The New York Times* (20 Oct 1942):20. For an excerpt from this article, see page 92 of the first edition of this book.

for this reason he purposely created lyrics that were "Masonic," whereas Sola's were "non-Masonic." Confirmation that Kernochan considered his lyrics to be Masonic comes from a subsequent edition of the "Finlandia" chorus undertaken by Galaxy in 1951, for which he changed certain words and phrases to produce a suitable version for non-Masonic use.[36]

Since the music for the Galaxy Music Corporation's 1951 edition of "Finlandia" is identical to that in the 1950 edition, it must have surprised Kernochan to receive letters from Sibelius and Sola in which he was criticized for the 1951 publication. In his letter of October 1951, Sibelius asked for a change in the musical notation and in the text (one word) as well. A copy of the "Finlandia Hymn" that showed the desired corrections was enclosed with Sibelius's letter.[37] Kernochan was particularly perplexed by this because what he had published was exactly the same piece of music authorized by the composer for the 1950 "Masonic" edition. Since Kernochan was quite ill at this point in time, he asked Kramer to acknowledge Sibelius's letter and explain that a more detailed discussion of the 1951 publication of *Finlandia Hymn* would follow.

In his reply to Sibelius that was written in December 1951, Kernochan apologizes for the use of two syllables on one note, which met with the composer's disapproval.[38] He then explains why he had to subdivide the half note into two quarter notes, namely, to accommodate the extra syllable in the English lyrics. He also reminds Sibelius that the subdivision of the half note occurred in the "Finlandia-Hymn" printed as the twelfth item of the 1950 edition of opus 113 and since this caused no objection from the composer during the editorial process for that edition, he wonders why it should now be a point of contention. After expressing his opinion as strongly as he dared with regard to the underlaying of the text, Kernochan graciously offered to accommodate the composer's wishes: "… my desire is to please you in all things and, if you definitely object to these measures, I shall gladly undertake the preparation of a new text at my earliest possible opportunity."

---

36  Sibelius's version of the "Finlandia Hymn" for unaccompanied male chorus (TTBB), with Kernochan's English lyrics, was published by Galaxy with a copyright date of 31 August 1951.

37  Letter from Jean Sibelius to Marshall Kernochan (12 October 1951) in KFC.

38  Letter from Marshall Kernochan to Jean Sibelius (7 December 1951) in the "Sibelius Family Collection 36/94," National Archives of Finland.

Shortly after Kernochan prepared his response to Sibelius's criticism, he received a letter dated 1 January 1952 from Wäinö Sola, which reiterated that same criticism. According to Sola, Sibelius had advised him "some time ago that he was not fully satisfied with the edition of the 'Finlandia Hymn' you sent him." Sibelius believed that Kernochan had "deviated from the notes as originally written by him" in measures 15 and 23. To help Kernochan make the necessary corrections, Sola enclosed with his letter a copy of "Sibelius's original notes." Sola not only requested that these changes be made, he also asked Kernochan to print his "Finnish text above the English in the final issue."[39]

Kernochan was true to his word. By 5 February 1952 he had prepared a new text that allowed the singing of a half note in the measure questioned by Sibelius and he enclosed this version with his letter to Sola.[40] This version, however, was never printed by Galaxy because sales of the first printing of the *Finlandia Hymn* were not overly successful and the need for a second printing never arose. Hence, both the 1950 edition and the separate choral edition of this musical composition remained essentially one and the same.

Ironically, it was the English lyrics created by Kernochan for the *Finlandia Hymn* that were requested by Einari Marvia in March 1952 for *Finland Sings*, a publication of fifty Finnish "folk" and "art"songs that was to include the "Finlandia" hymn. Marvia mentions that he intended to use the Finnish text by Wäinö Sola, who "has shown us your magnificent version in English. We would be much obliged to you if you will allow us to use your translation."[41] Presumably Kernochan gave his permission, for his lyrics appear in this song collection. His lyrics also appear in an appendix to the first printed edition in Finland of Sibelius's opus 113.[42]

---

39   Unfortunately, the original letter from Sola to Kernochan, with its enclosure of "Sibelius's notes," has not been located. What does survive is Sola's handwritten (undated) copy of the "Finlandia-Hymni," which includes the two verses of his Finnish lyrics. This copy survives among Toivo Nekton's papers [TFC]. It maintains the rhythm in measures 15 and 23 as originally written by Sibelius.

40   Letter from Marshall Kernochan to Wäinö Sola (5 Feb 1952) in KFC, which supposedly contained Kernochan's new verison of English lyrics for the *Finlandia Hymn*. A copy of this version of the lyrics is no longer extant among Kernochan's papers.

41   Letter from Einari Marvia to Marshall Kernochan (3 March 1952) in KFC.

42   See Jean Sibelius, *Rituaalimusiikki* (Helsinki: Suomi Loosi No. 1, 1968), 63, edited by Einari Marvia and published by the Grand Lodge of Finland. It contains a composite of pre-1950 versions of opus 113, together with some fraternal songs (such as the "Finlandia-Hymni") used at lodge meetings.

# CHAPTER EIGHT

## THE 1950 EDITION OF
### MASONIC RITUAL MUSIC

At the close of World War II, Sibelius once again became involved in providing music for the Masonic rituals of Suomi Lodge No. 1. His fellow lodge members suggested that additional pieces for voice and organ would enhance certain parts of the rituals and for that express purpose Samuli Sario had contributed two poems. Sario probably expected, or at least hoped, that his texts would be set to music by Sibelius, but he did not approach the composer on this matter. He left that part of the negotiation to Wäinö Sola.

On 1 October 1946 Sola took Sario's poems to Ainola and asked Sibelius if he would set them to music. Sibelius agreed and later that day began work on "Veljesvirsi" ("Ode to Fraternity") and "Ylistyshymni" ("Hymn").[1] Girded with inspiration, the composer worked all that evening and throughout the night. Early the next morning he telephoned Sola to come and get the completed scores. No doubt Sola was surprised to find that the 81-year-old composer still possessed the stamina to work in the same way that had been characteristic of him more than thirty years earlier. Sola was sufficiently impressed with this episode that he recorded it on a handwritten copy of "Ylistyshymni" as follows:

---

1    "Ode to Fraternity" and "Hymn" are the actual titles for these pieces in the 1950 English-language edition.

I received this song on 2. X. 46. It was probably composed the previous night. [JS2] telephoned me at 7 o'clock in the morning and told me to come and fetch it.[2]

Wäinö Sola and Ernst Linko gave the initial performance of these new pieces at Suomi Lodge No. 1, but before these additions to the ritual music could be copied for regular use by the lodges, Sibelius asked to have the scores returned to him. Apparently he wanted to make some changes and that is why the dates of composition are officially given as 16–17 December 1946 for "Ylistyshymni" and 20 December 1946 for "Veljesvirsi."[3] Both of these compositions underwent additional revisions in 1948. According to a notation in the score made by Sola, the last eight measures of "Ylistyshymni" were added in the summer of 1948.[4]

Before his final revisions to the ritual music were undertaken and before any formal negotiations were entered into with Kernochan for a second English-language edition, Sibelius drew up a "Deed of Gift" that granted to Suomi Lodge No. 1 certain rights.[5] What prompted Sibelius to formalize an agreement with his fellow Masons at this time is not known. Most likely he recognized that, with the addition of "Veljesvirsi" and "Ylistyshymni," his opus 113 was finally complete and therefore the time was right to put into writing what had previously been a verbal agreement with the lodge about the use of his opus 113. It is also possible that Suomi Lodge No. 1 initiated the idea of the "Deed of Gift" to insure that its members would not be denied use of the music after Sibelius's death. Whatever the reason, this "Deed of Gift" gave to Suomi Lodge No. 1 "full rights to perform the ritual music ... composed for it at different times, no matter whether this music is played in the lodge or outside

---

2　　Sola's notation appears on folio 3 of a "fair copy" (K. 1204) of "Ylistyshymni" that is in the Helsinki University Library. See also Kilpeläinen, *The Jean Sibelius Manuscripts at Helsinki University*, 345.

3　　Toivo Nekton confirms in a letter to Wäinö Sola (4 Feb 1949) that "Ylistyshymni" was composed on "16–17.XII.1946." For this letter, see KFC.

4　　Marvia, *Sibeliuksen Rituaalimusiikki*, 43, 202.

5　　The original "Deed of Gift," written in Finnish, is in the "Sibelius Family Collection 36/94," National Archives of Finland. A copy was made available to the author. A copy of the English translation of the original "Deed of Gift" was provided the author by Marshall Kernochan's son, John Kernochan. The English version of the "Deed" was typed and signed by the same persons who signed the original "Deed." It also bore the seal of the lodge and the signature of a person who certified "the accuracy of the copy." Marshall Kernochan had kept this copy of the "Deed" with other documents pertaining to the editions of opus 113.

it." It also entitled the lodge "to copy this music and ... give it to other home or foreign Freemasons' lodges for their ... rituals. If the music were ever printed in Finland or abroad, fifty (50) percent of any royalties were to be surrendered to the lodge to support its work." The document ends with "in other points the Royalty Act is to be followed." This "Deed of Gift," dated 8 October 1948, was signed by the composer at his home in Järvenpää. Immediately below his signature is a note of acceptance and thanks, signed in the presence of the composer on that same date by both the Grand Master and Grand Secretary of the lodge.

After receiving the "Deed of Gift," Suomi Lodge No. 1 copyrighted the ritual music by Sibelius in its possession and a certificate of copyright was filed with TEOSTO in that same year, 1948. The October 1948 copyrighted material, however, was soon to undergo further revision and within two years a new copyrighted edition authorized by Sibelius was available on both sides of the Atlantic. Nevertheless, the myth somehow persists that only the 1948 copyright filed in Finland carries the weight of legitimacy.[6] What has not been discussed in literature concerning the October 1948 copyright registered with TEOSTO and imprinted on the 1969 Finnish edition is that the music therein does not represent the *final* revisions Sibelius made before his death. Only the 1950 edition and its proof sheets carry those revisions!

Coincidentally, it was also in October 1948 that an exceptionally long and detailed article about Sibelius's *Masonic Ritual Music* was printed in *The New York Times*. It was by Noel Straus, who had received permission to write about the Masonic music from retired U. S. Navy Captain Maurice M. Witherspoon, director of public relations for the GLNY. Straus also credited Marshall Kernochan with the requisite historical data needed to write the article. Unfortunately, in the process of transferring data from Kernochan to Straus, a number of errors crept into the article. For example, Straus indicates 1923 was the year when Sibelius became initiated into the Craft and when the Grand Lodge of Finland was established, whereas the correct dates are 1922 and 1924 respectively. He cites 1935, instead of 1938, for the year when Sibelius received the Medal for Distinguished Achievement from the GLNY and states that the first "announced" American performance of the ritual music was in 1937 when, in fact, it was two years earlier in 1935.[7]

6    See, for example, Heineman, "Jean Sibelius," 10.
7    Straus, "Sibelius Score," *The New York Times* (3 Oct 1948):II, 7.

Straus begins his article by stating that it is highly unusual for a work by a well-known composer to elude the attention of his biographers. In fact, as far as he can tell, opus 113 has never been researched by musicologists, nor has the work been mentioned hitherto in print. Of particular interest is Straus's discussion of the non-Masonic versions of *Onward, Ye Peoples!* He not only draws attention to the orchestral accompaniment that Sibelius created for Channing Lefebvre's SATB version of this chorus but also indicates where the premiere performances occurred.[8] Even to this day, many Masons are unaware that this orchestration exists.

On the same day the Straus article appeared, George Sjöblom wrote a letter to Arvo Jacobson in Brooklyn in which he mentions that Rev. Bernhard Hillilä had asked for assistance in translating texts for a series of songs by Sibelius so that they could be published. Without specifically naming the songs, it is clear from the content of Sjöblom's letter that the songs were none other than those found in the first edition of opus 113. After explaining that he had already translated these song texts for Kernochan in 1935, Sjöblom informs Jacobson that the songs "in the English form are the property of the Grand Lodge of New York" and are copyrighted. Therefore "contemplated republication of them" would require consultation with both the GLNY and Galaxy as to "possible ethical and legal obstacles involved." Sjöblom's concluding paragraph begins: "I am at [a] loss to understand how the Masons in Finland could have relinquished these songs [to] others after they had been presented to the Masons [in New York]."[9]

No sooner had the "Deed of Gift" been signed by Sibelius in Finland than Toivo Nekton sent a letter to Marshall Kernochan, dated 11 October 1948, to inform him of what had transpired at Järvenpää.[10] Nekton explains that Sibelius "has made an assignment of his rights to the Grand Lodge of Finland—presumably relating only to the fraternal version." He then expresses his concern over this event, stating that "there should be a clarification by our Finnish brethren of the nature and scope of this arrangement between the

---

8   On the back cover of the orchestral edition (parts only) of *Onward, Ye Peoples!* can be found the following: "*Onward, Ye Peoples!* by Jean Sibelius was published on 9 February 1939. It was immediately chosen for performance at the Ann Arbor Festival, May 1939—Dr. Eral V. Moore, conductor—and the Worcester Festival, October 1939—Albert Stoessel, conductor."

9   Letter from George Sjöblom to Arvo Jacobson (3 Oct 1948) in SFC.

10  Letter from Toivo Nekton to Marshall Kernochan (11 Oct 1948) in NFC.

Master [Sibelius] and the Finnish Grand Body, so that we may be sure that nothing has been done which may confuse the copyright situation over here." Unfortunately, the assignment of rights did indeed confuse the copyright issue, as will be explained below.

In this same letter, Nekton tells Kernochan that at their next meeting he will bring with him the handwritten manuscript of opus 113 (MS-113-48tn) that he had recently received from Wäinö Sola. "This is supposed to have certain variations from the original which you have and I understand from Sola that the composer is contemplating other changes in it." Nekton was cautioned by Sola not to permit the score to be reproduced for circulation until those changes had been supplied by Sibelius.

The significance of these excerpts from Nekton's letter is twofold. First, it confirms that Nekton's copy of the manuscript was sent from Finland to New York at the beginning of October. Second, it reveals that when Sibelius assigned the rights for his ritual music (as it then existed in October of 1948) to Suomi Loosi No. 1, he had already prepared another version with the intention that it would supplant the one currently being used in Helsinki. Nekton concludes his letter by saying that "all of this is confusing to me" and he therefore would like to meet with Kernochan in order "to gain much light upon the whole subject of the ritual music."

At about the same time Nekton received his manuscript, Kernochan also received one from Sola, sent to him at his Galaxy office in New York City. The title page listed the work as "Ritual Music" and carried the same opus number assigned to the earlier versions of the score.[11] The manuscript (MS-113-48) consisted of eleven separate pieces: the eight found in the 1927 score, the "Finlandia-Hymni" in the TTBB version created by Sibelius and Sola in 1938, and the two pieces Sibelius had composed in 1946. Missing from the score was the chorale "Den höga himlen," which was not part of the original 1927 score but had been included as "No. 8" in the 1935 manuscript (MS-113-35). Ten of the eleven pieces in the manuscript were numbered, but the "Finlandia-Hymni," positioned on folio 17 between no. 7 and no. 8, had no number assigned to it. The entire score was dedicated to Wäinö Sola.

---

11  Sibelius's use of the same opus number to designate different versions of his Masonic ritual music has caused much confusion. At the very least, it would have been helpful if he had assigned opus 113 to the 1927 manuscript, opus 113a to the 1936 published edition, and opus 113b to the 1950 published edition.

Less than a month after the "Deed of Gift" was signed, Sibelius entered into direct negotiations with Kernochan, suggesting that a revised and expanded edition of his *Masonic Ritual Music* be published by Galaxy.[12] He also sent a letter directly to the Galaxy Music Corporation, expressing a similar desire to see a second English-language edition printed. Although the letter to Galaxy lacks a date, it seems, on the basis of content, to have been written at the same time as the letter to Kernochan.[13]

In the midst of the negotiations about the new edition, Sibelius let it be known that neither he nor the lodges in Finland had ever received copies of the 1936 edition of *Masonic Ritual Music*. Kernochan expressed astonishment at this news and hastened to explain to Sibelius, in a letter sent 8 December 1948, that the Grand Lodge of New York sent copies to Finland in 1937, as confirmed by surviving correspondence.[14] Apparently those copies never reached their destination, owing no doubt to the political and military turmoil in Europe at that time. In any event, Kernochan quickly remedied the situation. A shipment of the 1936 edition finally arrived in Finland on 1 February 1949, thereby allowing Sola to fully comprehend Nekton's suggestions about the desired order in which the pieces of the ritual music should appear. In his letter to Nekton of 19 February 1949 in which he thanks him for sending the printed copies, Sola conveys Sibelius's satisfaction with Kernochan's choral arrangements of Nos. 6 and 8, implying that he agreed to have them appear in the new edition.

Six months passed before Sibelius sent a brief reply to Kernochan's letter of 8 December 1948. The composer apologizes for the delay and then expresses his desire to have a contract for the printing of his Masonic music, forgetting that Galaxy was able to negotiate a contract only for non-Masonic publications. Sibelius writes:

> As for the Masonic music I think that in consideration of my posterity it would be best if we made up a contract according to the principles I have written to you before when telling you how pleased I was that my Masonic music is in so good hands. For me it is of the utmost importance that the music is published in its <u>definite</u> form. As for

---

12  Letter from Jean Sibelius to Marshall Kernochan (1 Nov 1948) in SSL.
13  Letter from Jean Sibelius to Galaxy Music Corporation, undated, in SSL.
14  See chapter three, in which Charles Johnson's letter of 3 June 1937 (in the SSL archives) is cited concerning the shipment of copies of the 1936 edition.

the nonmasonic [sic] editions it should be considered that Finland belongs to the Bern Convention.[15]

At approximately the same date of Sibelius's letter, additional correspondence from the Masons in Finland reached Nekton and Kernochan in which the question of having the Grand Lodge of New York enter into a contract with the composer were again addressed, all with an eye to securing royalties from the sale of a new edition of opus 113. On 31 July 1949, Kernochan wrote a letter to Nekton in which he expressed his dismay that neither Sibelius nor Eino Kyllönen "have quite understood the legal picture which the matter presents. And so we shall have to try to make clear to them the following facts." Several months later Kernochan wrote a seven-paragraph memorandum, in which he discussed those facts.[16]

While Sibelius was negotiating publication of an expanded edition of opus 113 with Kernochan, Sola was busy creating another handwritten copy of this same 1948 verison of the ritual music, only this time it was done as a favor to Arvo Aalto, Grand Master of SSL. Aalto had visited Iowa's Grand Lodge and Masonic Library in Cedar Rapids in 1947 and, while there, was asked by the librarian, Harry L. Haywood, if he could procure for the institution something autographed by Sibelius. Aalto thought it would be possible but delayed acting on the request, primarily because he wanted the autograph to be on a document the recipients would value. Not until Sibelius had Sola prepare the manuscript for Kernochan did Aalto get the idea of sending a duplicate, with the composer's autograph on the title page. Sola completed this second manuscript copy (MS-113-48io) on 15 December 1948. It was bound and sent to Iowa in April 1949 "with the compliments of the Grand Lodge of Finland."[17]

Sola, on his own initiative, managed to create havoc with copyright law by sending additional handwritten copies of the 1948 manuscript that he had

---

15   See letter from Jean Sibelius to Marshall Kernochan (30 June 1949) in KFC. Kenochan did draw up a preliminary contract that could have been used between Sibelius and the Grand Lodge of New York had the need for such a contract arisen. See Williams, *Sibelius and His Masonic Music* (1998), 109–110.

16   For more on this memorandum, see below.

17   A copy of MS-113-48io, as well as supporting information, was supplied by Joseph Nolte, Assistant Librarian of the Iowa Masonic Library. Excerpts from letters exchanged between Arvo Aalto and Harry L. Haywood are in Appendix I. Glenda Goss mistakenly states Noel Straus is describing this manuscript in his article "Sibelius Score," which appeared in *The New York Times* (Oct 1948). See Goss, ed., *The Sibelius Companion*, 279n1.

originally prepared for Kernochan, for in addition to the copy sent to Iowa, he sent copies to the Grand Lodges in Ohio, Massachusetts, California, and Colorado.[18] These manuscript copies had been promised as "thank you" gifts to those who had offered hospitality to Masons visiting form Finland.

In a letter written in Finnish to Nekton and dated 13 February 1949, Sola reveals the degree of confusion that existed in the minds of the Masons in Finland concerning the copyright and financial status of *Masonic Ritual Music*. On the very day his letter was written, Sola had visited Sibelius and he quotes the composer as saying that he "is particularly happy about the fact that the ritual music is beginning to receive its appreciation over there and that also practical financial matters are shaping so as to yield some return from these compositions." Sibelius's comment was made with reference to *Onward, Ye Peoples!* (a non-Masonic version of No. 6 of the 1936 edition) published by Galaxy. Sola mistakenly thought Sibelius was referring to the forthcoming publication of the whole of opus 113, causing him to write the following to Nekton: "As you know, Finland's freemasons will receive one half of the proceeds which the ritual music will yield. This part will be set up as a fund financing the prospective children's home. We have now made a good start and I believe in its future."

Nekton translated Sola's letter for Kernochan and added his own thoughts about the contents with these words: "I have no information about past arrangements regarding the 'financial matters' and 'yields' referred to by Sola. You will, of course tell me about that." The reason Nekton knew nothing about any financial matters or yields related to the ritual music is because none existed. At this date, only one item from opus 113 could generate royalties. That was No. 6, published as *Onward, Ye Peoples!* under a contractual agreement between Sibelius and Galaxy. That agreement initially net the fund for the orphaned

---

18    In his letter to Toivo Nekton of 19 February 1949, Wäinö Sola mentions he has sent handwritten copies to Ohio, Massachusetts, and California, but says nothing about Colorado or Iowa. Obviously Sola had not received Nekton's letter of 4 February 1949 before distributing his handwritten copies. In that letter Nekton told Sola "please do not send any manuscripts to any persons or lodges, because such advances would, or might, lead to legal complications." See also Nekton's letter of 23 February 1949 to Marshall Kernochan, in which he states "it will probably not take much diplomacy to straighten out this matter." Both letters are in KFC.

children's home $4,408.96 on 30 December 1948, the date when the first royalty check was sent to the Grand Lodge of Finland.[19]

The 1948 manuscript copies of opus 113 sent to Kernochan (MS-113-48) and to the lodge in Iowa (MS-113-48io) consist of forty-eight folios and are scored for voice(s) and "organo," but they do not contain any lyrics. Space normally reserved for the Finnish and Swedish lyrics was intentionally left blank. Sola knew Kernochan planned to provide a new set of lyrics in English for the entire opus and he decided to leave room for those lyrics to be added under the vocal parts. While this was a planned omission for the manuscript that made its way to New York City, it must have seemed a bit strange to those in Iowa who received a textless version of the ritual music.

Kernochan also thought it was strange that the manuscript he received lacked texts, a point he makes in a letter to Sibelius. Initially Kernochan thought the omission of texts was an oversight on the part of Sola, who had prepared the copy. When he mentioned the omission to Toivo Nekton, who was scheduled to prepare literal translations of the Finnish texts, he discovered the manuscript Nekton had received (MS-113-48tn) from Sola did indeed include those Finnish texts.[20]

After the receipt of the manuscript (MS-113-48) and Sibelius's communication to him in November, Kernochan moved forward in preparing the ritual music for publication by the GLNY. He had positive and negative photostats made of the manuscript. Two such sets are extant at LML and both lack the title page. These photostats are of particular significance, for they show how the manuscript looked when it first came from Finland. Only the positive set of photostats (C-113-48a), however, contains the *entire* manuscript. The

---

19  Several letters were exchanged in connection with the payment of this royalty check. They include: letter from Jean Sibelius to Marshall Kernochan (7 Dec 1948, in KFC); letter from Marshall Kernochan to Jean Sibelius (8 Dec 1949, in KFC); letter from A. Walter Kramer to Toivo Nekton (30 Dec 1948, in NFC); letter from A. Walter Kramer to the Grand Lodge of Finland (undated, in NFC); letter from Toivo Nekton to Eino Kyllönen (31 Dec 1948, in NFC).

20  Information about this extra manuscript sent to Nekton is in Marshall Kernochan's letter to Sibelius (8 Dec 1948) in the "Sibelius Family Collection 36/94," National Archives of Finland. What happened to Nekton's manuscript (MS-113-48tn) with the Finnish texts remains a mystery. It was not preserved at the Morton Lodge on Long Island, where Nekton had held membership, nor was it with his surviving papers preserved by his grandson, Roger Nekton. See Williams, *Sibelius and His Masonic Music: Supplement* (1999), 5.

negative set (C-113-48b) lacks several pages.[21] Although the manuscript (MS-113-48) itself is still preserved, it is no longer in its original form, for after it was received by Kernochan, changes were made to it. English lyrics were added, vocal parts were revised, and performance markings were inserted directly on the handwritten score.

Before Kernochan created his English lyrics, he must have sought the composer's advice, for Sibelius offers him the following suggestion in a letter dated 16 January 1949: "The text should be arranged according to American mentality, i.e., free and easy sung."[22] Kernochan's lyrics, based on a new translation of the Finnish texts by Toivo Nekton, were typed directly onto the manuscript folios.[23] Once they were in place, the vocal parts had to be revised to accommodate the prosody of the English language. This process usually involved a reduction in the number of notes required to set the individual syllables of the English words, just as was required in the revision of the vocal parts of the 1936 edition.

These so-called "extra" notes in the original score had to be eliminated. So effectively were the erasures made, the manuscript has to be held up to a bright light in order for them to be visible. What was used to make these erasures is not known, but whatever it was, it caused almost no damage to the manuscript. In those rare cases where an erasure of a note also caused a partial erasure of the original staff lines, those lines were carefully redrawn with a fine-point pen. It perhaps should be mentioned that these well-executed erasures are in stark contrast to the rather obvious ones made in the vocal part of the opening measures of "Veljesvirsi," erasures that were there when the manuscript was initially received in New York and they remained visible in subsequent photostats of that folio.

At present, it is not possible to determine whether the revision of the vocal parts was done by Kernochan and his staff at Galaxy or by Sola in consultation with Sibelius in Finland. The ink and style of writing observed in the revision process appear to match perfectly that of the original manuscript, and in the single instance

---

21   For a listing and description of the 1948 manuscripts, photostats, and other pre-publication material related to the second edition, see Appendix II.

22   Letter from Jean Sibelius to Marshall Kernochan (16 Jan 1949). John Kernochan provided the author with a copy of this letter. See Appendix I.

23   Nekton wasted no time in making literal translations of the compositions in the manuscript, as shown by the date of 10 December 1948 appearing above his signature on every one of the translations.

where a piece of music paper was pasted over a measure in the vocal part, the added piece of staff paper also seems to match the original paper. This suggests that the notational changes may have been made by Sola. If the vocal revisions were done in Finland, then the actual manuscript (MS-113-48), as well as photostats and proof sheets, may have made a number of transatlantic voyages.

Toivo Nekton and Wäinö Sola exchanged a number of letters in February of 1949 and all of them focused attention on the preparation of the new edition. In a two-page letter sent to Sola on 4 February 1949, Nekton reveals a number of points that have heretofore escaped verification. First and foremost, he mentions that he has enclosed a "photostatic copy of the entire revised repertory of Sibelius's Masonic ritual music with the revised English text. This has all revisions and additions by Sibelius, including 'Hymni' composed 16-17. XII.1946."[24] In this same letter, Nekton goes to great length to explain why he was not involved with the translation of the Finnish texts for the 1936 edition. It seems that at the time the first edition was being prepared, he was recovering from a nervous breakdown and declined to undertake the project. He continues with these words:

> Those translations were advised by George Sjöblom, whom you and I know to be a masterful student of the Suomian language. But, as you know, George is not a Mason. When I read these translations, I felt that many of them could be materially improved if the translator were one who could also reflect the Suomian texts with Masonic credo …
> I think you will agree that the new ones [translations] are somewhat more apt than the earlier [ones]. In some instances the changes are but very slight.[25]

In Sola's letter to Nekton of 13 February 1949, he includes some information that had been requested. For example, in his answer to Nekton's question as to whether or not the adaption of the English lyrics to the vocal line met with Sibelius's approval, Sola writes: "I am not able to exactly appraise the English texts, but would direct your attention to a couple of musical instances."[26]

---

24   Letter from Toivo Nekton to Wäinö Sola (4 Feb 1949) in KFC.
25   Ibid.
26   A translation of a letter from Wäinö Sola to Toivo Nekton (13 February 1949) and Nekton's comments about the facts and ideas express in Sola's letter were enclosed in a letter sent from Nekton to Marshall Kernochan (23 February 1949) in KFC.

Among those instances was one concerning the setting of the final word of
the text, "heaven" (in the last two bars of No. 4, Trio II). The point Sola made
about the text-music relationship caused Nekton to comment at length about
it to Kernochan, the nature of which shows that Nekton was more than a little
irritated by the situation. He wrote the following:

> He [Sola] has here picked an unworthy instance which hardly excuses
> his misgivings. He questions the singing enunciation of the word
> "hea-ven" in three full notes over the final span of three bars. His
> reasoning is obvious, even if not excusable. The Finnish nominative
> case of "heaven" is "taivas." In English we have two forms of the
> possessive case: "of heaven" and "heaven's." In Finnish no prepositions
> are used in declension; instead a noun is declined through fourteen
> cases, each identified by its specific affix added to the stem directly,
> or by dropping an intervening consonant (as in this case). Sola has
> in Finnish, therefore, only the affix-formed possessive "taiva(s)an"....
> Since Finnish is absolutely phonetic in pronunciation, Sola evidently
> feels that we should find some way of singing "of hea-ven" over those
> bars as he would sing "ta-ai-vaan."—Let's skip it.[27]

Another point Sola had made in his letter to Nekton that should not go
unnoticed is this sentence: "You may, consequently, procure copyright for this
latest ritual music in its present form(order) with its English text."[28] Since
the "present form" numbered but eleven pieces, Nekton informs Kernochan he
will "procure the assent of Sibelius (and Sola) to the printing of the combined
collection of all pieces heretofore submitted to you in such order as you think
proper, with the present English texts." In other words, the chorale "The lofty
Heav'n" (No. 8 of the 1936 edition) and the TTBB arrangement of the same
by Kernochan (No. 8a) were going to be printed in the new edition. Nekton
was merely going through the formality of asking the composer if this would
agree with his wishes.

The approach Nekton used to secure the composer's consent on the number
and sequence of pieces to be included in the 1950 edition was one that he
employed more than once in the course of printing the new edition. It was his

27    See letter from Toivo Nekton to Marshall Kernochan (23 February 1949) in KFC.
28    See letter from Wäino Sola to Toivo Nekton (13 February 1949) in KFC.

practice to have similar letters prepared, one in English from Kernochan and the other in Finnish from himself, and then have them mailed to Sibelius on the same date so that they would arrive together at Järvenpää. Nekton's reasoning in this instance was that "my letter will, perforce, sustain your suggestions, the combined effect of our letters will undoubtedly fetch a desirable solution and understanding in respect of the detail brought up in Sola's letters."[29]

There is no question the actual handwritten manuscript for the new edition of the ritual music (MS-113-48) was returned to Finland at least once for Sibelius's approval and revisions. After either Kernochan or Sola had aligned the vocal parts with the English lyrics, Sibelius reviewed the score and inserted a considerable number of editorial markings in the form of additions and corrections on the original handwritten manuscript. Surprisingly, not all of his markings were incorporated into the published edition of 1950 and therefore the manuscript in its third guise (MS-113-48c) becomes a very valuable document, for it is the *only* known source that includes them.[30]

In addition to the manuscript, at least one set of Galaxy's photostats (C-113-48c) also made a transatlantic voyage. This set represents the expanded and revised version of the 1948 manuscript. Its thirty-four pages arrange the twelve pieces in the order in which they ultimately appeared in the 1950 edition. In other words, the "Finlandia Hymn" has been moved to the end of the entire work and is now listed as item no. 12. The four-part *a cappella* chorale ("The lofty Heav'n"), which was included in the 1935 manuscript and subsequently omitted from the 1948 manuscript (MS-113-48), has been added here as item no. 11, with one important difference. It is now scored for solo voice and organ. Both numbers 6 and 11 have their respective choral (TTBB) versions included as numbers 6a and 11a.

No title page is provided, but the initial page of music carries the following statement of copyright: "Copyright, 1935, by Grand Lodge of Free and Accepted Masons of the State of New York. Revised Edition copyright, 1949, by Grand Lodge of Free and Accepted Masons of the State of New York." The reason 1949 appears here as the year of copyright is that Kernochan and his staff at Galaxy fully expected the edition to be published no later than

---

29  See letter from Toivo Nekton to Marshall Kernochan (23 February 1949) in KFC.
30  The various phases of the editorial process and the autograph markings of Sibelius are discussed both in chapter nine of the 1998 edition of Williams, *Sibelius and His Masonic Music*, and here in Appendix II

December of 1949. Kernochan may have wanted the edition published in time to honor Sibelius on his birthday, but the December date proved to be a bit too optimistic.

The thirty-four pages of this photostat copy are filled with four different sets of editorial markings: one in green ink, a second in red pencil, a third in blue/black ink, and the fourth in a black crayon or pencil. Although the names of the persons editing the score are not revealed, it is obvious that the hand using the black crayon belonged to Sibelius, so distinctive is the manner in which he makes his editorial markings. These can be readily found in the margins of the score. For example, whenever Sibleius wants to change a note, he usually draws a 5-line staff on which the note is correctly positioned. Directly below the staff, he supplies the letter name of the note and then draws a line from that note to the place within the score where the correction should occur.

Given the meticulous manner in which Sibelius entered his editorial changes, it would seem that he should only have had to mark a score once in order to have the corrections incorporated into the subsequent round of revisions. The photostats and proof sheets, however, reveal quite a different story. From them it is apparent that Sibelius sometimes had to enter the same editorial markings more than once before the editors at the Galaxy Music Corporation were able to produce an acceptable reading of the score.[31]

In an article written shortly after Sibelius's death in 1957, Sola makes reference to the numerous transatlantic exchanges of material that occurred before the 1950 edition could be published:

> When the second edition of Sibelius' ritual music was to be printed, the maestro wanted to check and revise certain passages. Kernochan, the English translator, also wanted to improve his translation. This resulted in an exchange of letters and notes of music for nearly two years, during which I experienced many difficulties in my capacity as go-between. Sibelius was very particular and exacting and permitted no arbitrary changes in the score.[32]

---

31   Sibelius habitually made extensive revisions of his works, even when he was engaged in the process of proof-reading. These proof sheets for opus 113 are valuable, not simply because they reveal the processes that led to the 1950 edition but, more importantly, because they contribute to the relatively small number of proof sheets that have *ever* been preserved for any of Sibelius's works.

32   Sola, "Jean Sibelius as a Composer of Freemason Music," 45.

Sola mentions that the exchange of letters and music spanned nearly two years. His statement is not quite accurate. The amount of time expended on the exchange and editing of the musical materials was limited to little more than a year, whereas the correspondence which Sola had with Toivo Nekton about the edition did extend over a much longer period of time. Sola and Nekton acted as "liaison officers" for Sibelius and for Kramer and Kernochan of Galaxy respectively. Their correspondence, in Finnish, amounts to more than two dozen letters and telegrams concerning the revision and publication of the expanded edition of Masonic music by the GLNY and Galaxy.[33]

Between 24 June and 19 July 1949, Kramer and Kernochan edited the "1st Proof" sheets (C-113-48f). Shortly thereafter, these proof sheets were sent to Finland. Sibelius again became directly involved in the editing process, using the broad heavy strokes of his pencil to make the necessary corrections. This set of proofs contained negative photostats of the entire score taped to larger sheets of paper measuring 10 ½ x 14 inches. The wide margins of these sheets allowed plenty of room for Kramer and Kernochan to write comments or questions to each other and even to Sibelius. For example, Kramer was concerned about the refrain for "Ode to Fraternity" (on page 25) and wrote the following message in the margin: "Professor Sibelius, we do not think this is correct, as it now appears. Please indicate how you wish it. A. W. K." Sibelius responded by crossing out the first and second endings of the "refrain" and moving the repeat sign to the final measure. To signal that he had answered the question, Sibelius took his pencil and crossed out Kramer's message. Kramer, however, had written his comments in green ink and therefore they are still legible despite Sibelius's attempt to obscure them.

On the final page of the score, Kramer again adds a message for the composer: "Prof. Sibelius: Please indicate more expression marks on this page unless you desire this piece to be sung <u>forte</u> throughout. A. W. K." This time Sibelius did not supply additional dynamic markings. Evidently he was perfectly satisfied to have "Finlandia" performed *forte* from start to finish.

A shipping label has been preserved from the exchange of musical materials across the Atlantic. This handwritten label, crudely fashioned from some graph paper and pasted onto heavy oiled brown wrapping paper of a type commonly used in the 1940s and 1950s, provides evidence that some material was sent directly from Sibelius's home in Järvenpää. At least one package, perhaps that

---

33    These letters are listed in Marvia, *Sibeliuksen Rituaalimusiikki*, 210–11.

containing the "1ˢᵗ Proof" described above, was shipped c/o the Finnish Consul General's office in New York City and then delivered by courier to the Galaxy Music Corporation offices[34]

Since the "1ˢᵗ Proof" sheets described above required a considerable amount of editing, additional sets of proofs had to be prepared before the score could go to press. Letters exchanged between Kramer and Sibelius provide a record of these transatlantic shipments of proofs, which occurred from 27 July 1949 to 5 October 1949.[35] Unfortunately, the final set of revised proofs has not been preserved at the GLNY nor is it known to be available from any other source. The reasons for this may be several, though the one that has the most credence focuses on Sibelius himself. It is worth noting that almost all of the musical materials leading up to the printing of the second edition, which Kernochan saved and donated to the Grand Lodge Library in 1951, contained autograph markings by Sibelius. If Sibelius had entered any editorial markings on any of the later proof sheets, Kernochan undoubtedly would have taken the trouble to preserve them as well. Apparently only the very last set of printer's proofs for the 1950 edition were not available to Sibelius for review. A reference to this is made in a letter Sibelius wrote to Kernochan from Järvenpää dated 16 March 1950: "I am sorry that I had no opportunity to read the last proofs."[36]

If the composer was not involved with the final proofs, does this mean that Sibelius suddenly decided to rely on the editors at Galaxy to correctly execute all of his editorial corrections, even though they had failed to do so in the past? That is doubtful. What is more likely is that Sibelius relied on Wäinö Sola to give final approval to the edition. Sola was in a position to do this, for he came to New York City in the fall of 1949 to present a series of recitals. One of his appearances was in the Grand Hall of the GLNY on 29 November 1949 when he sang, in Finnish, Sibelius's "Musique réligieuse" as originally

---

34   This information is in a letter from the Consul General to Galaxy (19 August 1949). The letter, found with the manuscript (MS-113-48) and other materials pertaining to the 1950 edition at the Utica Masonic Library, is now preserved at LML.

35   Letters from A. Walter Kramer to Sibelius (27 July 1949; 16 Sept 1949; 5 Oct 1949) are in the "Sibelius Family Collection 36/94," National Archives of Finland. A letter from Nekton to Sibelius (10 June 1949) announced that the first set of printer's proofs would soon arrive at Järvenpää.

36   Letter from Jean Sibelius to Marshall Kernochan (16 March 1950). John Kernochan provided the author with a copy of this letter. See Appendix I.

written in 1927.[37] Although there is only circumstantial evidence to support this idea, it nevertheless seems entirely plausible that Sola could have had the opportunity to meet with Kernochan, Kramer, and Nekton as many times as necessary to insure that the second edition would be printed according to the composer's intentions.

There is another bit of evidence that lends support to this idea that Sola had a hand in approving the final set of proofs. On the afternoon of 17 October 1949, Wäinö Sola, Janne Raitio (organist), and Paul Sjöblom visited Sibelius at Ainola. While there, Sola and Raitio performed several selections from opus 113.[38] In a 1996 telephone conversation with Raitio, Sjöblom asked if he could remember what portion of opus 113 had been performed on that October visit. Raitio recalled (he hoped correctly) that the selections were No. 5 "On kaunis maa" ("How fair are Earth"), No. 7 "Kella kaipuu rinnassansa" ("Who so ever hath a love"), and no. 8 "Veljesvirsi" ("Ode to Fraternity").[39] Whether or not these were the actual selections is perhaps of less importance than the fact that portions of opus 113 were performed shortly before Sola departed for America. If Sibelius had any last minute corrections or comments about the forthcoming edition, this visit would have provided him with the optimum opportunity for expressing them.[40]

Kernochan created several different versions of the foreword for the second edition before settling on that which ultimately appeared in print. At first, he considered making only minor changes to his foreword for the 1936 edition, but then he changed his mind and decided a more extensive foreword was needed. His initial revision of the foreword included the following statement about his role in creating the English lyrics: "In preparing the new English texts, the editor has also availed himself of the opportunity to revise and, he ventures to think, improve those which he wrote for the original edition." Here Kernochan gives himself credit for the new lyrics without the slightest hint

---

37  "Stated Communication for Nov. 29, 1949," *Transactions: The American Lodge of Research* V, no. 2 (May 1949–April 1951):196.

38  Paul Sjöblom, "How Sibelius Came to Smoke the Same Cigar with Me," 20–21.

39  Letter from Paul Sjöblom to the author (16 Sept 1996) contained this information.

40  Nothing disturbed Sibelius more than to allow one of his scores to be published before he had an opportunity to hear it performed. Such was the case with *Tapiola* (1926), which was commissioned and premiered by Americans in New York City. Sibelius therefore must have welcomed this meeting in 1949 because it allowed him to remain in control of final revisions based on a live performance.

that his work was based on the excellent English translations of the Finnish texts by Toivo Nekton.

Either Kernochan's conscience bothered him about this omission or, what is more likely, someone called his attention to this oversight. In any case, at the bottom of this printed sample of the foreword, Kernochan has written in pencil the following sentence, which was to be added after the sentence quoted above: "He has had the advantage of new and admirable translations made for him by that distinguished Mason and scholar, Toivo H. Nekton, whose helpful cooperation in this and other respects has been invaluable." This same sample page also contained another important change. The date of "November 1949" was crossed out in red ink and in its place was written "January 1950."[41]

Also expressed in Kernochan's preface to the 1950 edition was his opinion that "the *Masonic Ritual Music*, in the unanimous judgment of those who have heard it, takes rank with the master's best work. And we are confident that it is destined to be known and loved wherever Masons are met."

The second edition was published in the first week of January 1950 under both United States and international copyrights. Funds used to publish the second edition came directly from GLNY. Kernochan mentions this in the seventh section of a memorandum he sent to the Grand Secretary of GLNY on 9 January 1950:

> The publication has not been undertaken with any view to profit; it is, in fact, difficult to envision a time when Grand Lodge will have recovered its original outlay.

Kernochan actually wrote the memorandum mentioned above in the latter part of 1949. He prepared it for the benefit of Toivo Nekton in case Sibelius ever wanted to negotiate a formal contract with GLNY in reference to the second edition of his *Masonic Ritual Music*. In this two-page memorandum, Kernochan sets forth a number of facts that are pertinent to the publication of both the 1936 and 1950 editions. For example, he states that the English texts he wrote were presented to the GLNY as a gift and that only *Onward, Ye Peoples!* had been published by Galaxy for public sale by virtue of a special license from the GLNY. With this license Galaxy was permitted to negotiate

---

41    Several drafts of the prefatory page were with the other items pertaining to the 1950 edition
      materials found at the Utica Masonic Library.

"a royalty agreement directly with Sibelius," the only such agreement prior to the 1950s.

In a letter to Grand Master Frank Totten dated 9 January 1950, Kernochan includes the following paragraph:

> By the way, the last letter I have had from Sibelius mentions his desire to have a regular contract with Grand Lodge, which is of course the owner of record of the copyright, both U. S. and international. If he should write you on this subject I enclose a memorandum, originally prepared for the use of R∴W∴ Bro. Nekton, who was our "liaison officer" in this matter. I think this memorandum will give you all the data you want should it be necessary that Grand Lodge send him a letter. I am sending a copy of the memorandum to George [Irving] also.[42]

As it turned out, the officers of GLNY never had to rely on this memorandum for guidance in drawing up a contract with the composer because Sibelius apparently never asked for one.

Kernochan and the GLNY were especially careful to abide by copyright rules to protect the interests of Sibelius. The extant documents provide a number of examples of their legal protection. For instance, in September 1947, the New York Glee Club under the direction of Alfred Greenfield asked permission to borrow sixty copies of the 1936 edition for a broadcast performance of "Onward, ye Brethren!" The GLNY drew up a permission agreement, stating that the "Grand Lodge must continue to exercise all performing rights because of the conditions under which the music was originally received from the composer."[43] This particular broadcast occurred on 26 October 1947 and may have been the first occasion when the general public had a chance to hear a part of the ritual music in its Masonic form.

In the article Kernochan wrote for the *Masonic Family Magazine* to announce the publication of the new 1950 edition, he apologizes for not being able to send out advance copies of the music. He explains that the Masonic organizations are "most justly entitled to receive the same, but this cannot be done until the

---

42  Letter from Marshall Kernochan to Frank Totten (9 Jan 1950) at LML. A copy of the memorandum was attached to this letter.
43  Letter from Wendell Walker to Alfred Greenfield (11 Sept 1947) at LML.

copyrights have been secured."[44] Although this article appeared in the March-April 1950 issue of the magazine, it was submitted for publication in the latter part of 1949, prior to the January 1950 date when a certificate of copyright was filed in Washington, D.C.[45] This article is of singular importance, however, for Kernochan's statement about the manuscript Sibelius sent to GLNY to create a new English-language edition, a portion of which is quoted below.

> This newly revised and enlarged version was recently sent us directly from the composer, who informs us that it is the final and finished form of the music, and supersedes the original edition. Naturally it is the duty as well as the pleasure of Grand Lodge to comply at once with his wishes. Accordingly, the original version must now be considered obsolete. The final and definitive version, including the new numbers, with texts revised and adapted by the writer, and from proofs read and approved by Sibelius himself, will be published by Grand Lodge in the fall under United States and international copyright.[46]

The key phrases—"the final and finished form of the music"; "supersedes the original edition"; and "the original version must now be considered obsolete"—clearly express the composer's wishes. Admittedly, it must have been, and still may be, difficult for Masons in Finland to accept the fact that the Americans and not the Finns were to have the honor of presenting to the world the "definitive form" of Sibelius's opus 113, a work that had occupied the composer's attention over the course of almost a quarter of a century.

---

44    Kernochan, "Sibelius Masonic Ritual Music," 15.
45    A copy of the copyright certificate is at LML.
46    Kernochan, "Sibelius' Masonic Ritual Music," 15.

# CHAPTER NINE

## The Years 1950–1970

Frequent exchanges of correspondence between Jean Sibelius and members of the GLNY did not come to an end with the publication of the 1950 edition of *Masonic Ritual Music*. Greetings sent from the Grand Master of the GLNY to Sibelius on the occasion of his birthday had become a regular occurrence and this tradition continued until the composer's death in 1957. In response to greetings conveyed by Grand Master Frank M. Totten in December of 1949, Sibelius sent a note (typed) of thanks from Järvenpää.[1] George Irving, Grand Secretary of the GLNY, forwarded Sibelius's note to Marshall Kernochan, thinking that he might like to keep it for himself. Kernochan, however, thought better of that idea. In a letter to Irving, he thanked him for sending "the greatest little note from Sibelius" and returned it to him for safe keeping. At the bottom of this typed letter, in Kernochnan's hand, is written: "I also enclose carbon of my letter to Sibelius being sent to-day."[2] That carbon (copy) no longer exists at LML, but the very mention of it indicates that there was much more correspondence with Sibelius than is presently available for study.

Perhaps Sibelius's note cited above prompted Kernochan to suggest that the Grand Lodge send, with its compliments, a dozen copies or so of the new edition to the composer. He thought "it would be one of those little acts which are always so greatly appreciated."[3] George Irving lost no time in acting upon Kernochan's suggestion. On 1 February 1950 he informed Sibelius that he would soon receive a dozen copies, adding that "it was a great pleasure to send

---

1   Letter from Jean Sibelius to Frank Totten (10 Jan 1950) in LML. See Appendix I.
2   Letter from Marshall Kernochan to George Irving (8 Feb 1950) in LML.
3   Letter from Marshall Kernochan to George Irving (27 Jan 1950) in LML.

them along with our appreciation and thanks for the beautiful gift that you have made to the Grand Lodge of the State of New York."⁴

Advertisements for the revised and expanded edition were placed in non-Masonic as well as Masonic publications, even though the music could be purchased only from the Grand Secretary at the GLNY by duly accredited Masons. These advertisements made known that a contemporary Finnish composer had written "fine music for the three degrees of the Blue Lodge, … used by several of the Lodges in the State of New York," but they were short on specific details. They gave neither the name of the publisher nor a specific address where copies of the music could be purchased.

Loren W. Adair, organist for the Compass Lodge (No. 590 F. & A.M.) in Pomona, California, had read about the new edition in the *Etude Music Magazine* and was eager to introduce Sibelius's music into his lodge work. He wrote to the GLNY to find out how he might obtain the score and in that same letter of 20 February 1950 he also asked for additional information about "appropriate music for both the Blue Lodges as well as the upper bodies in the York Rite."⁵ At the time of Adair's inquiry, copies of the first edition could be had from the Grand Secretary's office for $1 and those of the "new and definitive edition" for $1.50.

On 16 March 1950 Sibelius wrote to Kernochan, thanking him for his recent letter and for the very kind preface to his "Ritual Music," but saying nothing about the score itself. It is conceivable that a copy of the new edition had not yet reached Järvenpää. The third paragraph of Sibelius's letter, however, is particularly interesting for it indicates that the composer was very eager to have individual items from his *Masonic Ritual Music* published separately by Galaxy. It further demonstrates that he continued to be satisfied with his previous contractual arrangements with this publisher.⁶

Kernochan was also eager to have music from the new edition performed beyond the confines of Masonic lodges. As he had done in the 1930s, he once again looked for ways to bring some of the numbers from the score into the realm of non-Masonic use. One of his first written expressions of this idea

---

4    Letter from George Irving to Jean Sibelius (1 Feb 1950) in LML. See Appendix I.
5    Letter from Loren Adair to GLNY (20 Feb 1950) in LML.
6    Letter from Jean Sibelius to Marshall Kernochan (16 March 1950). A copy of this letter was made available to the author by John Kernochan and is reprinted in Appendix I.

occurs in a postscript to a letter sent to Grand Master Richard A. Rowlands on 5 July 1950:

> P.S.—Don't forget that we are hoping at Galaxy to receive that permissive letter from you with regard to the Sibelius music. I think it efficiently protects Grand Lodge from the sightest [sic] chance of having the music fall into alien hands. We are all ready to go ahead, and are confident that it will bring in a piece of change for the old boy.[7]

What parts of the ritual music Kernochan wanted to publish are not mentioned, but on that same date of 5 July 1950 Rowlands wrote an official letter to Galaxy Music Corporation in which he gave his permission "to publish, for public sale, any number or numbers from the 1950 revised edition." His letter further states that Sibelius would "receive all royalties accruing from said publications, as in the case of 'Onward, ye Peoples!' previously published under a similar arrangement." An undated draft of this letter was apparently shown to Kernochan for his comments and approval, for at the bottom of the draft, in Kernochan's hand, is written an addendum to the final paragraph: "except by written permission of the then Grand Master at the time of such transfer. This may be withdrawn at any time on previous notice."[8] The official letter sent to Galaxy on 5 July 1950 contains the additional words suggested by Kernochan.

Within two weeks of the granting of this "permission to publish," Sibelius had signed a contract with the Galaxy Music Corporation for publication of the instrumental pieces (nos. 1 and 10) from the 1950 edition of *Masonic Ritual Music* as organ transcriptions prepared by Channing Lefebvre. These transcriptions were issued under the titles *Prelude* and *Funeral Music*.[9] The following year Sibelius signed a similar contract with Galaxy for publication

---

7   Letter from Marshall Kernochan to Richard Rowlands (5 July 1950) in LML.
8   Draft of a letter, with addendum by Marhsall Kernochan, and the official letter from Richard Rowlands to Galaxy Music Corp. (5 July 1950) in LML.
9   Sibelius signed the contract on 17 July 1950. A copy of the contract is in the "Sibelius Family Collection, 36/94," National Archives of Finland. When Kramer sent Sibelius the contract, he asked the composer to please sign it in ink. No doubt this request was necessitated by the fact that Sibelius liked to use a heavy dark pencil for many of his editorial corrections as well as for his signature on letters he had previously sent to Kramer, Kernochan, and Nekton.

of his own arrangement of the "Finlandia-Hymni" for male chorus (TTBB).[10]
All three pieces were to be published under the same terms as were negotiated
for *Onward, Ye Peoples!*

A month later Toivo Nekton wrote to Richard Rowlands, summarizing his
understanding of a discussion they had had several months earlier on 22 May
1950 with Juho Kuosmanan, Senior Warden of the Grand Lodge of Finland.
Of particular interest are the fourth and fifth paragraphs:

> The subject is, as stated, the request of the Finnish Grand Lodge for
> a contribution of $15,000 by its mother Grand Lodge of New York
> toward the foundation of a Masonic Home for Orphaned Children
> in Finland, to be known as "The Sibelius Home for Children."
>
> It is to be so named after R∴W∴ Jean Sibelius, who has already
> donated to its realization half of the proceeds from his "Masonic
> Ritual Music" which was in 1935 presented to, and copyrighted
> and printed by our Grand Lodge. He has pledged half of all similar
> proceeds to the same cause.[11]

The amount of money which Nekton was asking the GLNY to contribute
to the orphanage was considerable in terms of the buying power of a dollar in
1950, but it was not beyond the realm of possibility, considering what Masons
had been donating for similar projects closer to home. Ever since the 1890s,
Masons in the United States had focused attention on providing excellent
facilities to care for widows and orphans. One of the prime examples of how
well the Masons had been providing this care can be observed at the Masonic
Home in Utica (NY), a facility that has been in existence for over 100 years.[12]
Whether or not the GLNY contributed the amount requested by Kuosmanan
in 1950 is not known. The orphanage, however, did come into being and carried
the Sibelius name.

In addition to the issue of Masonic charity toward a war-torn country,
Nekton's letter raised the issue of money generated from the sale of the 1936
edition of *Masonic Ritual Music*. While it has always been known that Sibelius

---

10   This contract was issued 12 April 1951, but Sibelius did not sign it until 16 May 1951.
     A copy of the contract is in the "Sibelius Family Collection, 36/94," National Archives of
     Finland.
11   Letter from Toivo Nekton to Richard Rowlands (7 August 1950) in LML.
12   The facility is now known as the Masonic Care Community.

received royalties from the various non-Masonic versions of *Onward, Ye Peoples!* published by Galaxy, this may be the sole example of a written statement about the composer receiving the "proceeds" (not royalties) from the Masonic versions of his music published under the jurisdiction of the GLNY. It is worth noting that financial statements concerning the printing costs and sales of the first (1936) edition of opus 113 were sent to SSL as soon as they were available, the implication being that any "proceeds" (meaning "profits," not "royalties") accruing from sales would be shared with Sibelius and his fellow Masons.[13]

For a period of about a year during World War II, Finland was considered by the United States and Great Britain to be an enemy country and this resulted in the curtailment of royalty payments to Sibelius. Finland was removed from this "enemy" list before 1945, but royalty payments did not immediately resume. The hardships that Sibelius and his family were experiencing because of unpaid royalties from sales and performances of his scores, coupled with the inflationary eroding of the composer's state pension, came to the attention of his British colleagues and friends. When they tried to remedy the situation by staging several benefit concerts, Sibelius strongly objected. He did not wish to appear privileged while his fellow countrymen were also suffering the ravages of war.

On 5 April 1945, George Axelsson of Stockholm informed *The New York Times* of the growing severity of Sibelius's wartime privation. Two days later, the newspaper carried an article about royalties owed to the composer, together with a reprint of the cable which the Philharmonic-Symphony Society had sent to the composer on the previous day: "The Philharmonic-Symphony Society of New York as an expression of gratification to you for the many great works it has been privileged to offer its audiences desires to remit to you an additional royalty payment of $1000."

As the war drew to a close, the United States government began to ease some restrictions which had been placed upon the transfer of money to Finland. Under the new rules, amounts of $500 or less could be paid directly to individuals without having to go through government channels. This meant the Philharmonic-Symphony Society was allowed to circumvent all of the red tape imposed by the Washington (DC) bureau handling foreign royalty payments. In compliance with these rules, the additional royalty payment of $1000, made

---

13  For a discussion of the financial aspects of publishing the first edition, see chapter 3.

possible by an anonymous donor, was sent to Sibelius in two separate checks of $500 each.

Neither the end of the war nor the attention given in the news to Sibelius's financial dilemma brought an end to the composer's problems in collecting royalty payments. Sometimes the transfer of funds from the United States to Finland was delayed by circumstances beyond the composer's control. For example, a 1948 letter from the Grand Secretary Eino Kyllönen to Carl H. Claudy of the Masonic Service Association in Washington, D.C. asks that the payment of funds to a bank in New York City be postponed because SSL did not currently have an account with that particular institution.[14]

Well into the 1950s *The New York Times* was still reporting on the composer's plight.[15] In the center of the controversy were his publishers in Berlin (Breitkopf & Härtel) and Copenhagen (Hansen) who together held more than 200 of the Sibelius copyrights, along with one of his publishers in New York City (Associated Music Publishers). Galaxy was not named in the newspaper articles, yet it was Galaxy and the GLNY that continued to be the focus of a royalty dispute that Einari Marvia and other Masons in Finland raised concerning opus 113. The evidence, however, seems to suggest that Galaxy and the Masons of the GLNY were very meticulous in executing their obligations with regard to "royalties" and "proceeds" owed to the composer.

In the opening paragraph of a letter to Marshall Kernochan dated 16 January 1949, Sibelius writes:

> Please accept my best thanks for your kind letter and the Royalty Statement. I can see from it that my "Onward Ye Peoples" is in good hands. I am very satisfied with the result and I only hope that your publishing house could take all my Masonic music as well as the non Masonic. As you already know, Brother Kyllönen has received the amount.[16]

---

14   Letter from Eino Kyllönen to Carl H. Claudy (22 Nov 1948) in the SSL archives. A copy of the letter was made available to the author.

15   See, for example, the following articles in *The New York Times*: Olin Downes, "Plight of Sibelius" (2 July 1950):II, 6; "Plight of Sibelius Confuses Capital" (10 July 1950):16; Olin Downes, "Copyright Triangle" (30 July 1950):II, 6.

16   Letter from Jean Sibelius to Marshall Kernochan (16 Jan 1949). A copy of this letter was made available to the author by John Kernochan and is reprinted in Appendix I.

This letter confirms that royalties due Sibelius were paid by Galaxy directly to Eino Kyllönen at SSL. Other sources indicate that these monies were subsequently deposited in the Finnish Masonic Benevolence Fund.

Sibelius, of course, was kept fully informed of his royalties because Galaxy sent him annual reports. For example, a letter dated 5 June 1952 informed "Professor Sibelius" that Galaxy had "sent a check in the amount of $492.24 to SSL in care of Eino Kyllönen for royalties … for … 'Onward, Ye Peoples!' for the year 1951." Along with the letter was enclosed a royalty statement.[17]

Wäinö Sola, however, seemed unaware that Galaxy had been making royalty payments to the SSL fund over an extended period of time. In a letter (1 January 1952) to Kernochan concerning Galaxy's new edition of the "Finlandia Hymn," Sola adds this comment:

> In case you are not fully aware of the fact I use this opportunity to advise you that our M∴W∴ Brother Sibelius is donating 50 percent of the total income he receive [sic] from printing of his Masonic music to the Finnish Masonic Benevolence-fond [sic] for orphan children.[18]

Sola's comment seems peculiar, at best, since the plans for founding the Sibelius Home for Children and the composer's donation of 50% of his royalties toward that goal had been known to those associated with Galaxy and the GLNY for quite some time.[19] These plans were also known to Masons living in Brooklyn's "Finntown." In an article that chronicles the history of their Finlandia Masonic Club, the authors mention that *Onward, Ye Peoples!* became an immediate best-seller and as a consequence earned "a considerable amount in royalties which were sent to Northern U-Bank for the Children's Home founded by Jean Sibelius."[20]

In light of the care with which Galaxy reported and paid the royalties due the composer for this single composition, it is unfortunate that information given

---

17   Letter from A. Walter Kramer to Jean Sibelius (5 June 1952). A copy of this letter was made available to the author by the Helsinki University Library.
18   Letter from Wäinö Sola to Marshall Kernochan (1 Jan 1952). A copy of this letter was made available to the author by Helsinki University Library.
19   See, for example, the August 1950 letter cited above from Nekton to Rowlands.
20   Emil L. Ostman and Willy W. Rutzy, "25 Years of Finlandia Masonic Club" (printed ca. 1980):2. A copy of the article is in SFC.

in a *New York Times* article by Olin Downes has been used to support criticism of the GLNY and the very publishing house that had Sibelius's interests at heart. The article in question appeared 2 July 1950. It quoted at length an "on the scene" interview with Sibelius by Paul Sjöblom in which the composer was asked if there were any truth to the statement that he had not received so much as a single penny of his American royalties for performances of his works. Sibelius replied that indeed he had not received "a penny."[21]

The way this 1950 article was worded, it gave the impression that this was the first time Sibelius had publically expressed his distress over non-payment of royalties. Such, of course, was not the case. Complaints about unpaid royalties were made by the composer in the late 1930s, prompting Marshall Kernochan to respond to them. In a letter to George Sjöblom of 26 May 1938, Kernochan asked that the composer be informed (in Finnish) why many of his works might not qualify for royalty payments:

> He says that he has never received compensation from the presentation of his works in America. I wonder if he realizes that works which are not copyrighted are in what is known as the public domain and that any one can publish and perform them gratis? This is the case with a large number of Mr. Sibelius's compositions and the American publishers who have issued and sold these works were not infringing in doing so.[22]

A few Masons in Finland have quoted the line "I have not received a penny" from the 1950 article cited above to undergird their contention that Sibelius was owed royalties from both the 1936 and 1950 published editions of his ritual music. This of course is not true. First of all, Sibelius made his remarks to Paul Sjöblom with respect to performance, not publication, royalties. Secondly, Sibelius did not enter into any formal contract with the GLNY for publication of his opus 113. Further, the GLNY may never have realized any substantial profit from the publication of either the 1936 or the 1950 editions and, in the case of the 1950 edition, probably sustained a loss, since no anonymous donor came forth to fund that edition as had been done for the earlier one.

---

21    Downes, "Plight of Sibelius."
22    Letter from Marshall Kernochan to George Sjöblom (26 May 1938) in SFC.

Shortly after the Grand Secretary of the GLNY sent a dozen copies of the new edition to Järvenpää, Wäinö Sola ordered another 100 copies for distribution among the lodges in Finland, but he never received them. Sola mentions this in a 1952 letter to Kernochan and asks that his request be filled as quickly as possible.[23]

Whether or not this particular request was acted upon cannot be verified from surviving documents. It is known, however, that the GLNY supplied well over 100 free copies of the 1950 edition between 1950 and 1974. From the correspondence that is available for study, it seems that shipments from New York to Helsinki of both the 1936 and 1950 edition did occasionally "go astray." To cite but one example, a 1974 letter from Wendell Walker to Paavo Heikkila contains the following paragraph:

> What I want to assure you immediately is that I am sending one-half dozen copies of the 1950 edition of the music, and am holding an additional supply in case this first lot should go astray. There will be no charge.[24]

Sibelius's plan to turn over half of his royalties to help fund an orphanage bearing his name was well intentioned, but the revenue raised was not always sufficient to support the operation. This meant that his Masonic brothers had to find additional sources of revenue to financially support this fledgling institution. To that end, Sola and his fellow Masons in Helsinki finally came up with a plan to sell a limited number of autographed copies of the 1950 edition of *Masonic Ritual Msuic* at greatly inflated prices.

In the latter part of 1954 when Sola was Grand Secretary of SSL, he ordered 50 copies of the new edition from the GLNY. These copies were shipped at the beginning of 1955, but the cost of the copies and the shipping were not charged to SSL. Instead, Marshall Kernochan paid the bill and the copies were sent *gratis*. In the summer of 1955, Sola sent 20 of those copies to Sibelius for his autograph. Upon their return to Sola, the SSL sold them at 9,800 (old) Finnish marks each. The remaining 30 copies were sold at 1,000 (old) Finnish marks each, bringing in a combined total of 226,000 FM. This scheme worked so well that another sale of the second edition was held in 1965, albeit without

---

23    Letter from Wäinö Sola to Marshall Kernochan (1 Jan 1952), cited above.
24    Letter from Wendall K. Walker to Paavo Heikkila (3 June 1974) in LML.

autographed copies, to mark the 100th anniversary of the composer's birth. SSL contacted the GLNY in March of 1964 and placed an order for 50 copies, and once again the copies were donated free of charge. These 50 copies were sold for 50 (new) Finnish marks each.[25]

The orphanage in Helsinki was not the only institution that would bear Sibelius's name. By the time Sibelius celebrated his 90th birthday in December of 1955, his name had already graced the title of several different civic and cultural endeavors in his homeland. For example, the name of the Conservatory of Music in Helsinki was changed to the Sibelius Academy early in 1939, at a time when Ernst Linko was its director. Sibelius also allowed his name to be given to a Foundation established by the Society of Finnish Composers in 1945 during the Society's first year of operation. The purpose of the Sibelius Foundation was to help underwrite the creation of new compositions by Finnish composers. In appreciation for lending his support to the Foundation, Sibelius was named the first honorary member of this Society.

Other examples include the establishment of the Sibelius Medal, an award to be given annually to a prominent composer from any part of the world. In 1950 Sibelius became the first recipient of the medal, which was made from gold mined in the northern part of Finland and inscribed with "Jean Sibelius, Music is the Light of My Life." In June of 1951, "The Sibelius Week," one of Finland's most famous music festivals, was inaugurated in the Great Hall of Helsinki's University. Although the festival has continued to the present time, it no longer bears the composer's name, which was dropped in 1965 when the event was expanded from one to three weeks. One need only list a few more examples such as the Sibelius Prize, established in 1958 with Dmitri Shostakovich its first recipient, and the Sibelius Violin Competition to appreciate the all-pervasive influence Sibelius has had and continues to have in the musical life of Finland.[26]

For at least two decades, musical organizations and civic groups had held celebrations honoring Sibelius on his 70th. 75th. 80th, 85th, and 90th birthdays. News of the public celebrations in Finland and the United States

---

25   Marvia, *Sibeliuksen Rituaalimusiikki*, 205.

26   Only one Masonic lodge outside of Finland is permitted to carry the composer's name. That is the Sibelius Lodge, No. 1167 of F. and A. M., which meets in the Doric Room of GLNY. This Sibelius Lodge was constituted in June of 1965, the year marking the 100th anniversary of the birth of its namesake. See Arvo E. Lainen, "The Birth of Sibelius Lodge" contained in the program for the Ceremony of Constitution.

were usually noted in *The New York Times*. The awarding of honors for Sibelius and performances of his music by major orchestras were traditional means used to mark each of these five-year milestones in his career. Noticeably lacking from all these news accounts was any mention of Sibelius's connection with Freemasonry or any indication that the Masons in New York City were also involved in these birthday commemorations.

The GLNY had its own way of marking these occasions. The Grand Master would send official greetings to Sibelius in Järvenpää and the Grand Lodge Library and Museum located in the GLNY building would organize exhibits of music and artifacts owned by the Masons, which were associated directly with Sibelius, his family, and his homeland. The exhibits of 1950 and 1955 included the 1935 presentation copy of the "Masonic Ritual Music," a metal casting of a sculptured head of Sibelius from an original by the Finnish sculptor, Hjalmar Steinholm, photographs of Sibelius with his wife, children, and close friends, and examples of Finnish handcrafts such as a Finnish wall rug and wooden candlesticks carved in the traditional "Kalevala period" design. In 1955 a brief program was held in the Grand Lodge Library to officially open the exhibit. Several dignitaries spoke, the Finnish baritone Kalle Ruusunen sang (unaccompanied) "Onward, ye Peoples!" and a recording of *Finlandia* opened and closed the program.

A different kind of 90th birthday celebration for Sibelius was held in Manchester, England, on 22 November 1955. On this date the first performance in England of the entire 1950 edition of *Masonic Ritual Music* was given at the Manchester Lodge of Masonic Research.[27]

Not all of the music performed by and for Masons in New York City took place within the walls of the GLNY. On 12 April 1953, the Masonic Symphony Orchestra of 75 musicians gave its first public concert at Carnegie Hall. The program included a Beethoven concerto, a Dvorak symphony, a Glinka overture, and Sibelius's *Finlandia*. A review of the concert printed the following day noted that *Finlandia* was played because Sibelius was a Mason.[28]

While this was indeed the premiere concert for the Masonic Symphony Orchestra, it was by no means the first concert in New York City by a symphony

---

27    Arthur Sharp, "Sibelius's Masonic Ritual Music," *Ars Quatuor Coronatorum* 75 (1962):8. In this article, the contents of the 1950 edition of opus 113 is listed incorrectly, nos. 5 and 6 being reversed except for the names of the poets.
28    "Masonic Symphony Plays," *The New York Times* (13 April 1953):31.

orchestra comprised solely of Master Masons. As early as November 1932 plans were initiated by New York Masons to found the Universal Symphony Society.[29] The purposes of the Society, as listed in the by-laws, were: to organize and maintain choral groups; to provide orchestral and other musical entertainment for Masons, their families, and friends at moderate cost; to employ the artistic talents of Masons whenever possible; to contribute monies raised from concerts to Masonic charity and relief funds; to contribute to the musical education of all children at the Masonic Home in Utica; and to defray the costs of musical training for children who showed artistic promise.[30] Though not stated in the by-laws, a most important aspect of this new organization was to provide employment for musicians who undoubtedly were adversely affected by the Depression of the 1930s.[31]

The inaugural concert of the 100-member Universal Symphony Society orchestra occurred 12 May 1934 at the Mecca Temple in New York City. Included on the program was Sibelius's *Finlandia* along with works by Beethoven, Liszt, and Mozart. Also featured was Arthur Anderson of the Metropolitan Opera.[32] The committee responsible for launching this successful venture informed fellow Masons that the Universal Symphony Society was intended to "carry into practice, for purposes not only cultural but also beneficent, Freemasonry's teaching that music is one of the highest spiritual joys and one of the most ennobling influences in the lives of men."[33] Less than two years after this statement was written, Sibelius presented GLNY with his gift of ritual music.

The composer was to outlive two American friends who had faithfully championed his music, Olin Downes (1886–1955) and Marshall Kernochan (1880–1955). A concert performed in Carnegie Hall on 4 December 1955 by The Symphony of the Air served a dual purpose: it was given in honor of Sibelius's 90th birthday and in memory of Olin Downes. On this special

---

29   See memorandum of 2 November 1932 from Charles Johnson to Christopher Mollenhauer in the "Symphony" file in LML.

30   S. v. "Symphony" file in LML.

31   Communication from the Music Committee of the Grand Master (18 September 1933), 1. S. v. "Symphony" file in LML.

32   The commemorative program booklet contains the names of the performers, a short history about the music of Masonry and about the newly formed Universal Symphony Society, program notes, etc. The Mecca Temple was located at 131 West 55th Street. S. v. "Symphony" file in LML.

33   Communication from the Music Committee of the Grand Master (18 September 1933), 3.

occasion the orchestra was conducted by Sibelius's son-in-law, Jussi Jalas of Helsinki.

In September of 1957, when death finally came to the composer, the people around the world mourned his passing.[34] The Grand Secretary of the GLNY sent the following message to SSL on 24 September 1957:

> Please accept condolences and deep sympathy of the Grand Master and the Grand Lodge of the State of New York on the passing of Jan Sibelius, a great man. His influence in Masonry and throughout the world through his music is a great loss to country and fraternity.[35]

During Sibelius's lifetime, the frequency with which his opus 113 was used in connection with degree work in American lodges is difficult, if not impossible, to determine. In fact, it might be safe to conclude that, aside from the instrumental numbers, only "Onward, ye Brethren" and "The Lofty Heav'n" were ever sung on a regular basis. These were the two vocal numbers selected for inclusion in *Sing … Brothers, Sing*, a very popular songbook published in 1940 and designed for both ritual and social use by Masons.[36] Where one might expect to find the most frequent use of the ritual music is in lodges with membership drawn from the Finnish immigrant community, such as the Eureka Lodge of Manhattan, but there is no documentation to support this supposition.

What can be documented are the half dozen or more programs held between 1935 and 1952 on the occasion of a "Stated Communication" of the American Lodge of Research. One such event occurred in 1940 when the Bruno Huhn Quartet performed a concert for members of the American Lodge of Research. The first half of the program was devoted to Masonic works by Johann Naumann and the second half to Sibelius's opus 113.[37] Another occurred on 29 November

---

34  Paul Sjöblom wrote a letter from Helsinki to his father, in which he describes how he learned of the composer's death. For an excerpt from this letter of 21 September 1957, see Appendix I.

35  Telegram from Edward R. Carmen to Lauri Sarkin (24 Sept 1957) in LML. This expression of condolence was later printed in "Sibelius…Composer…Freemason," *The Empire State Mason* 5 (Holiday Issue 1957):18. The printed version used Jean, instead of Jan, for the composer's given name, and changed the final words to "his music will live forever."

36  Price, ed., *Sing…Brothers, Sing* (New York: Gettinger Printing, 1940):46–49, 51.

37  Kernochan, "Craft Music on Program for Lodge of Research," *Transactions: American Lodge of Research* (April 1950):151.

1949 with Wäinö Sola as the featured guest artist. He performed a recital of Sibelius's music that included the whole of opus 113. Sola's appearance at the lodge was arranged in conjunction with one of his American concert tours.[38] One more example was the program held on 29 April 1952 that featured the Quartette of St. Cecile Lodge and organist Albert Boyce. Before the assembled group of thirty-six Masons, the Quartette "rendered a complete set of selections of Masonic music, ... some 14 numbers in all."[39] Obviously both the solo and quartet versions of "Onward, ye Brethern" and "The Lofty Heav'n" were included if fourteen numbers were performed that evening.

Programs featuring Sibelius's ritual music could be heard in places other than lodge halls, but they were usually restricted to Masonic members. For example, the Finnish Masonic Club of New York sponsored a concert on 14 November 1959 at the Park Avenue Methodist Church on 86th Street in New York City. Performing were Finnish musicians, Matti Lehtinen (an operatic tenor) and Janne Raitio (organist), and their program consisted solely of opus 113. The announcement for this concert stated that "although admittance to the Sibelius concert is for [Finnish] Master Masons exclusively, our F. M. C. Ladies Auxiliary will arrange a 'De Luxe' table of refreshments for this superb occasion after the program."[40] Lehtinen and Raitio were in New York not only as performing artists but also as part of a visiting delegation of Finnish Masons acting as a "Ritual or Degree Team." In this latter role, they were to present the Fellowcraft Degree in the Finnish language at the Eureka Lodge, "the first time that a Masonic Ritual Degree could be heard in Finnish in its entirety in America."[41] Here was at least one occasion for which Sibelius's music might well have been performed with the original Finnish lyrics.

The interpretation of opus 113 by Matti Lehtinen and Janne Raitio can be heard on a 1962 recording made in the Lauttasaari Church of Helsinki. This recording, with the lyrics sung in Finnish, was commissioned by Suomi Lodge No.1 to commemorate its 40th anniversary. Nine years later, Matti Lehtinen

---

38  "Stated Communication for 29 Nov 1949," *Transactions: American Lodge of Research* V, no. 2 (May 1949-April 1951):196.

39  "Stated Communication for 29 April 1952," *Transactions: American Lodge of Research* V, no. 3 (April 1951-Jan 1952):312.

40  "Distinguished Visitors from Humanitas Masonic Club to be Presented in New York," *New Yorkin Uutiset* (23 Oct 1959):3.

41  Ibid.

made another recording of the ritual music with the English lyrics.[42] Since 1971, several more recordings of the ritual music have been made in Finland as well as in Italy, Germany, and the United States.[43]

A decade after Sibelius's death, the question of royalties from the 1936 and 1950 editions of *Masonic Ritual Music* continued to come up for discussion. The Grand Secretary of SSL, Martti Mustakallio, wrote to his counterpart at the GLNY, Wendell Walker, on 3 May 1967 and asked that he contact Olavi Munkki, the Finnish Ambassador in Washington.[44] Walker complied with the request and, following his telephone conversation with the Ambassador, he sent Mustakallio a letter from which this excerpt is taken:

> As explained to the Ambassador, I do not anticipate any real difficulty in coming to an understanding about the Masonic ritual music. The concern of our Grand Lodge from the beginning was to make the music available for Masonic purposes while protecting it from non-Masonic circulation.[45]

Walker then proceeded to clarify how the 1935 manuscript came to GLNY, namely, "as a gift from your Grand Lodge and not from Suomi Lodge No. 1 or from Waino Sola." As further clarification of the matter, Walker enclosed photostats of the original "gift" manuscript and provided lengthy quotations from a personal letter exchanged between Arvo Aalto and Charles Johnson in March of 1935 and from the preface of the 1936 published edition. Obviously the letter concerned copyright and royalty agreements, but since a copy of Musstakallio's letter is not available from either the GLNY or SSL archives, it is impossible to reconstruct the essence of the controversy.

Although questions of copyright continued to be discussed among members of the Masonic community in Finland, the matter for the GLNY soon became one of purely academic interest. As early as the mid-1960s, Sibelius's opus 113 was not being used in the GLNY ritual. Walker confirms this in a letter dated

---

42  [Einari Marvia], "The Ritual Music of Sibelius," [typescript], 16. For the 1971 recording, Lehtinen dubbed English lyrics over the organ accompaniment heard in the earlier recording.

43  For a list of known recordings of opus 113, see the Discography listings.

44  Letter from Martti Mustakallio to Wendell K. Walker (3 May 1967). A copy of this letter was in the SSL archives in the 1970s but has since disappeared.

45  Letter from Wendell K. Walker to Martti Mustakallio (13 May 1967) in LML.

29 March 1968, which he wrote in response to an inquiry from a fellow Mason in Arizona concerning the use of Sibelius's music.[46]

Letters requesting information about purchasing copies of the *Masonic Ritual Music* were received by the GLNY from the far corners of the United States and abroad, and from this correspondence it is possible to gauge the interest in, if not the use of, Sibelius's opus 113. In 1963, for example, Alvin Langdon Coburn of Rhos-on-Sea in the northern part of Wales ordered copies of the 1950 edition. Upon receipt of his order, he wrote to the GLNY expressing his pleasure with the music.[47]

In stark contrast to the waning of interest in Sibelius's Masonic music in New York after the composer's death, SSL and Suomi Lodge No. 1 were inspired to enrich the legacy that had been given them and to see that this music would continue to serve a vital part in the workings of the Craft. The death of Sibelius meant that the authorized version published in 1950 would forever remain a musical treasure. To insure that this treasure would endure in the composer's homeland, SSL organized a music committee in 1966 to arrange for a Finnish publication of opus 113 with words in Finnish, Swedish, German, and English. The committee, headed by Einari Marvia, brought forth this edition in 1969. Although it appeared *after* the second American edition, it does *not* present the post-October 1948 version of opus 113 found in the second (English-language) edition copyrighted in 1950.[48]

In celebration of the 130th anniversary of Sibelius's birth, three special public concerts were organized by the Sixth Manhattan District of the GLNY in October of 1995, each devoted to the composer's music. Musicians from Finland were invited to perform chamber music concerts in Utica (NY) and Alexandria (VA). A third and final concert, held in the Grand Hall of the GLNY, was performed by the New York Metamorphoses Orchestra, with soloists Jaakko

---

46   Letter from Wendell K. Walker to R. J. Wheeler (29 March 1968) in LML.
47   Coburn's initial correspondence with the GLNY has not been preserved, but the contents of his first two letters can be surmised from a third letter in LML from the GLNY to Alvin Langdon Coburn (21 Nov 1963). It acknowledges receipt of Coburn's letters and makes reference to their contents.
48   A revision of the 1969 edition appeared in 1992. See Reinikainen, "Masonic Ritual Music in Finland," 4. For a discussion of the differences between the Finnish and American versions of opus 113, see Appendix II. The 1969 Finnish edition was provided with a supplement that offers to lodge musicians other compositions by Sibelius that can be incorporated into ritual or fellowship activities. This supplement, however, should not be mistaken for an *authorized addition* to opus 113.

Kuusisto (violin) and Martti Miettinen (tenor). Sibelius's Masonic music (opus 113) was included on each of these three programs. The 1927 Finnish version in eight sections for voice and organ was performed in Utica and Alexandria. The 1940 orchestrated version of these same eight sections by Leo Funtek was presented in New York City.[49] For many Masons and non-Masons alike who attended these concerts, this was their very first encounter with Sibelius's opus 113.

Membership in Masonic lodges of the United States has declined appreciably in the past two or three decades, thereby making it difficult for even a Grand Lodge to garner enough talent or interest to perform some of the "classical" music created for degree work. If it were not for recordings of the *Masonic Ritual Music*, many current members would never come to know the hauntingly beautiful music that Sibelius created for Freemasonry. These recordings, along with the published editions of opus 113, also permit those who are not Masons to experience what was for Sibelius a very personal and introspective part of his life and career.

---

49   These performances of opus 113 were recorded live in the concert halls and released in a
     CD format, accompanied by a commemorative booklet. See the Discography listings.

# *EPILOGUE*

During the period which has become known as "the silence of Järvenpää," Sibelius tried to live a very solitary life. For too long he had been subjected to what seemed to be endless intrusions into his privacy by tourists and news-hungry correspondents. Even those who were privileged to visit him between 1927 and 1957, Olin Downes and George Sjöblom among them, could not resist trying to penetrate that "silence." What was uppermost in the minds of everyone in the music world was, of course, the mystery surrounding the composition of a new symphony that had been promised to more than one conductor for a premiere performance. When this work did not come into being, even though there were many reports to the contrary, the rumor spread that Sibelius had simply stopped composing altogether. Perhaps that is why so few took notice of anything Sibelius composed after 1927, or if they did, they assumed the works were of little significance.

It is therefore all the more interesting to note that during twenty-five of the so-called thirty years of "silence," Sibelius was occupied with composing, orchestrating, arranging, revising, and editing all or parts of opus 113. Obviously he considered this work to be more than just a grouping of musical miniatures, more than just a musical aid to Masonic rituals. Opus 113 had become for him an expression of his belief in the universality of the Divine, a belief given credence in the beauty and wonder of nature. Though he was not a fervent or frequent participant in the workings of the Craft, his initiation into Freemasonry had awakened in him an awareness of one's inescapable pilgrimage towards the "Light." That may be the reason why he initially chose to title his 1927 musical gift to Suomi Lodge No. 1, "Musique réligieuse."

# APPENDIX I

The following documents are reprinted here with the kind permission of the owners and may not be reproduced in whole or in part without their consent.

1. Letter from Arvo A. Aalto of SSL (6 March 1935) to Charles H. Johnson of the GLNY. Paragraphs 1–4 of the letter are quoted below [LML of GLNY, owner]:

   Dear Br. Grand Secretary:
   Slightly more than one year has elapsed since you wrote me concerning the ritual music composed by R∴W∴ Bro. Jean Sibelius. You may have thought, that this matter has elapsed from my mind, but that has not been the case. The matter has been under preparation during all this time, although a suitable time or occasion for making the request to our famous composer has not appeared before recently. The compositions had been dedicated to the Suomi Lodge here with the reservation, that they were not to be used anywhere else. Therefore the composer's consent had to be obtained.
   I am now more than delighted to be able to advise you, that a complete set of all these compositions is now on the way to New York. It is certainly a great pleasure and privilege to all of us to be able to send you something of our own to show our appreciation and our sincere feelings. It is so much more pleasing, when this music is one of our biggest assests [sic], which we are happy and proud to own. We are indebted to your Grand Lodge for so many favours and kindnesses, that we appreciate every occasion to be able to reciprocate within our small powers.
   May I also add, that there is to my knowledge only one more complete ritual music in the whole world. No wonder we are proud of having these compositions.

Although the Finnish and Swedish text appears on every composition, I have enclosed in a separate envelope six copies of the texts in both languages. We are unable to have good translations made up here; some of the songs, I am sure, have already been translated into English. No doubt you will be able to get the rest translated without any greater inconvenience. This will make the content more enjoyable for the members of your Lodges.

2.   Citation read in English for the awarding of the Grand Master's Medal to Sibelius at the GLNY ceremony (May 1938). A copy of the same in Finnish (translated by G. Sjöblom) was sent to SSL for the actual presentation of the medal to Sibelius. The full citation appears below [LML of GLNY, owner]:

R∴W∴ Jean Sibelius, loyal and distinguished citizen of Finland, and foremost of contemporary musical composers, the Grand Lodge of Free and Accepted Masons of The State of New York confers upon you its special Grand Master's medal for outstanding achievement in the art of Music. You have preserved with peculiar power, in these modern days of confusion and surrender to things transitory and tawdry, the true spirit of the bards of old who caught the echoes of eternal truth and sent them vibrating through the world on the wings of musical sound. Your art is the most subtle of all and through it soul speaks most directly to soul. Commanding the resources of the modern orchestra, you have nobly expressed the rhythmic pulsations of the universal mind and you have particularly revealed to the world the glory of your native land and its people. Master of technique, you have resisted the temptations of mere virtuosity and, listening to the promptings of your own inner nature, have given to the world undying music of simple dignity, breadth and poetic charm. An honored officer of the Grand Lodge of Finland, your brother Masons of the Empire State of the Western World hail you as a man of unswerving integrity, a brother of patient courage, and the composer of the most inspiring symphonic music of our time.

3.   Letter [typed] from George Sjöblom in Brooklyn, NY (3 Oct 1948) to Arvo P. Jacobson in Brooklyn, NY. Excerpts quoted below [SFC, owner]:

Dear Mr. Jacobson:

Rev. Bernhard Hillilä asked me to assist in translating the enclosed songs which you had given him, together with the music by Sibelius.

The words of these songs are not unfamiliar to me, for I translated them in 1935 (or perhaps it was in 1936) for Mr. Marshall Kernochan of 7 Sutton Place, New York City, president of the Galaxy Music Corp. of New York, who was then—and perhaps still is—a high-ranking official in the Masonic order.

The enclosed clipping from The New York Times of Oct. 3 will show without further explanation on my part that these songs in their English form are the property of the Grand Lodge of Masons of New York State.... Therefore it seems to me that any contemplated re-publication of them—if such is the purpose—by any other organization would require consultation with the Grand Lodge of Masons....

I am at [a] loss to understand how the Masons in Finland could have relinquished these songs ... after they had been presented to the Masons. Be that as it may, it seems to me that translating these words all over again would be unnecessary inasmuch as the English words are already obtainable from the source above referred to.

4. Letter [typed] from Jean Sibelius in Järvenpää (16 Jan 1949) to Marshall Kernochan in New York City [KFC, owner]:

Dear Brother Kernochan,

Please accept my best thanks for your letter and the Royalty Statement. I can see from it that my "Onward Ye Peoples" is in good hands. I am very satisfied with the result and I only hope that your publishing house could take all my Masonic music as well as the non Masonic. As you already know, Brother Kyllönen has received the amount.

The text should be arranged according to American mentality, i.e. free and easy sung.

Thanking you once more I remain, with kindest regards to Mr.
Cramer [sic] and to yourself, Yours fraternally,

5.  Letter from Jean Sibelius in Järvenpää (10 Jan 1950) to Frank Totten of the
    GLNY [LML of GLNY, owner]:

    For your very kind congratulations on the occasion of my eighty-
    fourth birthday please accept and convey to the Brethren my most
    cordial thanks. I was very happy to receive your greetings.
    With kindest regards,
    Fraternally yours,

6.  Letter from George Irving of the GLNY (1 Feb 1950) to Sibelius in
    Järvenpää [LML of GLNY, owner]:

    Dear Brother Sibelius,
    Under separate cover, we are sending you one dozen copies of the
    new set of the Masonic Ritual Music.
    It is a great pleasure to send them along with our appreciation and
    thanks for the beautiful gift that you have made to the Grand Lodge
    of the State of New York.
    With our best wishes to you,

7.  Letter [typed] from Jean Sibelius in Järvenpää (16 March 1950) to Marshall
    Kernochan in New York City [KFC[, owner]:

    Dear Brother Kernochan,
    I have received your letter of February 9th and thank you most
    cordially for it as well as for the very kind preface you have written to
    my Ritual Music.
    I am sorry that I had no opportunity to read the last proofs.
    If the Grand Master should give his consent to publish any of the
    numbers for public sale, I would be glad to have them published by
    the Galaxy Music Corporation under the same terms as "Onward
    you [sic] Peoples."
    With my kindest regards,
    Cordially and fraternally,

8.  "Memorandum by Marshall Kernochan. For reference in case R∴W∴ Jean
    Sibelius should at any time desire a written contract with Grand Lodge
    with reference to this Ritual Music." This document is not dated, but is
    known to have been formulated before 9 January 1950 for use by Toivo
    Nekton in any future negotiations with Sibelius. It consists of 8 separate
    items, of which only nos. 6 and 7 are reprinted below [LML of GLNY,
    owner]:

    (6) When commissioning Galaxy to print for them the new and
    definitive edition, Grand Lodge was under the necessity of immediately
    taking out both United States and international copyrights, in order
    to protect the music and texts from theft and piracy in other countries
    as well as our own, pending other subsequent arrangements which
    might be concluded. Consequently Grand Lodge is the sole party
    empowered to execute any contract regarding the Masonic versions
    of this music; or of the non-Masonic versions, except in case they
    might grant a license to some publishing firm, in which case the
    contract would be between the publishing firm and R∴W∴ Brother
    Sibelius. Of course, no such license would ever be granted without
    the written authority of R∴W∴ Brother Sibelius. Should he, or the
    Grand Lodge of Finland desire at any time to arrange for publication
    in other countries, it would be a simple matter to communicate
    with Grand Lodge, who would most certainly be only too happy to
    cooperate in any respect.

    (7) Since the Masonic versions of this music are sold by Grand Lodge
    exclusively to duly accredited Masons and for Masonic purposes only,
    the market is obviously an extremely limited one. The publication
    has not been undertaken with any view to profit; it is, in fact, difficult
    to envision a time when Grand Lodge will have recovered its original
    outlay.

9.  Letter [typed] from Toivo H. Nekton (7 August 1950) to Richard A.
    Rowlands, Grand Master of GLNY. Paragraphs 5-8 are quoted below
    [LML of GLNY, owner]:

The subject is, as stated, the request of the Finnish Grand Lodge for a contribution of $15,000 by its mother Grand Lodge of New York toward the foundation of a Masonic Home for Orphaned Children in Finland, to be known as "The Sibelius Home for Children."

It is to be so named after R∴W∴ Jean Sibelius, who has already donated to its realization half of the proceeds from his "Masonic Ritual Music" which was in 1935 presented to, and copyrighted and printed by our Grand Lodge. He has pledged half of all similar proceeds to the same cause.

In making this appeal, our Finnish Brotherhood is duly mindful and sincerely appreciative of the great assistance heretofore accorded to them by our New York Grand Lodge in the past several years. I am in a peculiar position to demonstrate that, with our moral and material support in the past quarter-century, the Finnish Masons have not only made the American <u>democratic</u> system of Freemasonry a potential moral factor for abiding courage and resuscitation of civic life in their own country, but that the effects of their achievements stand to inspire, by example, the Old World fraternities to a more realistic practice of the Freemasonic Creed in this crucial period of mankind.

Many requests for financial aid have come to our Grand Lodge from European fraternal organizations in countries where national self-determination is yet as uncertain as in the long past. Of course, these applications have been based on urgent humanitarian grounds. But I purposely use the distinctive adjective "democratic" in respect of Finland, because in her case, as I will show, we have not, nor shall, "cast (our) bread upon the waters" in vain.

10. Letter [typed] from Toivo H. Nekton (7 August 1950) to Richard A. Rowlands, Grand Master of GLNY [S. v. "Nekton" file at LML]:

Most Worshipful Sir:

After I wrote you my letter of June 29th and before I received your kind response of July 6th, I became immobilized at home with blood poisoning in my left foot. I had, indeed, begun to frame in long hand this present letter—the one I mentioned in the last paragraph of that of June 29th. I hope its delay may not put you to inconvenience.

Anant the visit of R∴W∴ Bro. Juho Kuosmanan of Finland and the writer with you at 11:45 A.M. on Monday, May 22, 1950, the following particulars are respectfully presented in further explanation of the subject then briefly discussed.

Bro. Kuosmanan is the Senior Grand Warden of the Grand Lodge of Finland and, as his credentials, presented to you, show, is authorized by his Grand Lodge and by its Grand Master, M∴W∴ Gunnar Jaatinen, to deal in all respects with the subject matter of his visit.

I hope you will bear with the copious frame of this letter because, after its reading for your own information as Grand Master, you will want to submit it to your Committee on "Foreign Correspondence and Relations" which, in due course, will convey its recommendations to you. However, before you do so, I hope that I may discuss the subject with you [during] a summer visit, as I have requested.

The subject is, as stated, the request of the Finnish Grand Lodge for a contribution of $15,000 by its mother Grand Lodge of New York toward the foundation of a Masonic Home for Orphaned Children in Finland, to be known as "The Sibelius Home for Children."

It is to be so named after R∴W∴ Jean Sibelius, who has already donated to its realization half of the proceeds from his "Masonic Ritual Music" which was in 1935 presented to, and copyrighted and printed by our Grand Lodge. He has pledged half of all similar proceeds to the same cause.

In making this appeal, our Finnish Brotherhood is duly mindful and sincerely appreciative of the great assistance heretofore accorded to them by our New York Grand Lodge in the past several years. I am in a peculiar position to demonstrate that, with our moral and material support in the past quarter-century, the Finnish Masons have not only made the American <u>democratic</u> system of Freemasonry a potential moral factor for abiding courage and resuscitation of civic life in their own country, but that the effects of their achievements stand to inspire, by example, the Old World fraternities to a more realistic practice of the Freemasonic Creed in this crucial period of mankind.

Many requests for financial aid have come to our Grand Lodge from European fraternal organizations in countries where national self-determination is yet as uncertain as in the long past. Of course, these applications have been based on urgent humanitarian grounds. But I purposely use the distinctive adjective "democratic" in respect of Finland, because in her case, as I will show, we have not, nor shall, "cast (our) bread upon the waters" in vain.

I sincerely apologize for the length of this letter, as I am well aware of the many and endless problems of your grand office. But with equal sincerity I dare hope for a favorable reaction on your part and on the part of our Grand Lodge authorities to this appeal of the Grand Lodge of Finland.

Awaiting your kind call for a stop at Schenectady, I am, Most truly yours,

11. One of the most moving of all letters in the Sjöblom Family Collection is that which George Sjöblom received from his son Paul, dated 21 September 1957. Paul Sjöblom, who at the time was residing in Helsinki, describes how he learned of Sibelius's death. An excerpt from this letter is quoted below, with permission [SFC, owner]:

> This letter is being written with a heavy heart. Yesterday morning I received your letter about Uncle Sergei's death. Then in the late evening came the shocking tidings of Sibelius' sudden passing. It was all the more shocking to me because only the day before Martti Similä had dropped over to see me and suggested he telephone Sibelius. I stood beside Martti when he put through his call and I heard Sibelius' voice plainly. It was a strong, masculine voice, which did not falter a bit or betray any sign of senility or illness or even fatigue. Sibelius was in a good mood and when Martti asked him how he felt, the response was "erinomaisesti!" We were both happy to note that the master was evidently in excellent condition. Dr. Ylijoki, his physician, is quoted today in the *Helsingin Sanomat* as saying Sibelius' death came as a surprise because he had been in good health

all fall and had been feeling well yesterday morning. Besides, he had never suffered a hemorrhage before.

The way I learned the news was strange. We had been visiting the Kahmas, who are now near neighbors of ours here at Lauttasaari. We left just before 11 p.m. As soon as we entered our car, I turned on the radio. The "Swan of Tuonela" was being played. It gave me a weird presentiment. I found myself thinking: "Sibelius is dead." Then I tried to console myself by remembering the phone call of the day before. "Nonsense, how could he be dead? He was so full of life yesterday," I forced myself to think. The piece was still being played when we reached our house. I shut off the car radio but hurried indoors to turn on our house radio in my room. My thought was that I must find out why the "Swan of Tuonela" was closing the day's radio program. I was sure it had some significance. The last strains faded away. Then Count Creutz's voice said, "Nämä Tuonelan joutsenen sävelet tuovat viestin säveltä jämestari Jean Sibeliuksen kuolemasta."

I immediately called up the *Uusi Suomi* to find out more … I learned that the news of Sibelius' death had been received as late as 10:15 p.m.—too late to be announced in connection with the last news broadcast of the day. So the announcement was made at the close of the day's program, at 11 p.m. I got the few details that were known and put in a call to the *Daily Express* in London. I was connected before I could properly finish the first sentence of my brief story. I improvised the rest. Then I called the NBC. (This morning, early, a cable came from Allen, chief of the TV news and features, asking that I cover the funeral with my movie-camera.) Next I banged out a story for the Chicago *Tribune* …

# APPENDIX II

1. The various manuscripts, photostat copies, and editions of *Masonic Ritual Music* (opus 113) in the Robert Livingston Masonic Library of the Grand Lodge of New York are described below. Each has been given a reference number for the purposes of identification in the text.

MS-113-35      The handwritten "gift" manuscript copy of opus 113 presented to GLNY in 1935 that contains 9 musical numbers. Manuscript written on 10 1/2 x 13 1/4 music paper with imprint of R. E. Westerlund-Helsinki. 30pp Outer title page: Masonic Ritual Music/composed for/the Grand Lodge of Finland/by/R∴W∴ Bro. Jean Sibelius/*respectfully Jean Sibelius*. Inner title page: Masonic Ritual Music/composed by/R∴W∴ Bro./ *Jean Sibelius*. Has signature of Jean Sibelius on both the outer and inner title pages. Manuscript bound in leather. [Note: this bound manuscript, which contains many errors (as indicated below in comments about C-113-35), was returned to the Grand Lodge in Finland sometime after 1998 per that lodge's request.]

C-113-35      A photostat copy made of the manuscript cited above (MS–113–35) on 8 1/2 x 11 sheets. A note on the cover states that it represents a corrected copy: "The original presentation copy of this work, from the Grand Lodge of Finland, contains a very large number of errors and omissions. No performance should be given without comparing the sheets used with this copy, in which all corrections are indicated in <u>red</u>, <u>above</u> the staves." Signed by Marshall R. Kernochan. 24pp. (Omits some of the pages used as "title pages" before individual numbers of MS-113-35, hence six pages are omitted.

C-113-36    The 1936 published edition prepared by Marshall Kernochan and printed for GLNY by the Galaxy Music Corp. Titled *Masonic Ritual Music.* Copyright: Contains 9 numbers plus TTBB arrangements of no. 6 and of no. 8. No. 8 is scored for SATB. [When the copyright for this edition expired in 1963, Sibelius's wife and children renewed the copyright, which expires in 2010.]

C-113-40    Photocopy of the handwritten orchestral score completed by Leo Funtek "21 June 1940." Funtek, with Sibelius's authorization, orchestrated the 8 pieces of the 1927 version of opus 113. His score, however, includes a number of changes that were later incorporated into the 1950 edition of opus 113.

MS-113-48   Handwritten manuscript prepared by Wäinö Sola in [November] 1948 and sent to Marshall Kernochan at New York City. No lyrics supplied; includes 11 pieces. Title page: To Wäinö Sola/Ritual Music/F. & A. M. of Finland/Jean Sibelius/op. 113/M. S. Copyrigth [sic]. Written on No. 10 paper with imprint of Fazers Musikhandel, Helsingfors. 23pp. Only a photostat copy shows this manuscript in its original form; it is extant at GLNY, represented by C-113-48a. The original MS-113-48 was altered when English lyrics were added, necessitating changes in the melody and rhythm of the vocal line. See description of MS-113-48c.

C-113-48a   Photostat (positive) of MS 113-48 before any alterations were made to accommodate the English lyrics or before any editorial marks were supplied by Sibelius. In other words, as far as can be determined, this photostat is the sole example of how the MS-113-48 looked when first prepared by Wäinö Sola in 1948 and sent to Kernochan. No lyrics supplied; lacks title page; begins on page 2 and ends on page 24 (each page given a separate sheet). In MS-113-48 no number was assigned to the "Finlandia-Hymni" on folio 17. This photostat, however, shows a "No. 11" added before the title with a fine point pen. The hand that wrote in this number appears to be the same as the one that wrote all of the other numbers in the 1948 manuscript, namely that of Wäinö Sola.

C-113-48b    Photostat (negative) of MS-113-48 before any alterations to the score were made; no lyrics; lacks title page and pages 2, 5, 7-9, 18-19. Shows "No. 11" written on folio 17 before the title, "Finlandia-Hymni," and thus this photostat is identical to C-113-48a with respect to the extant pages. On the cover of a large envelope containing this photostat is written: Sibelius-Masonic Ritual Service/1948-November/Negatives.

MS-113-48c    This handwritten manuscript (MS-113-48), prepared by Sola in 1948, underwent alteration when English lyrics were typed into the score, causing the rhythmic and melodic contour of the vocal parts to be changed to fit those lyrics. Sent back to Finland for editorial revisions by Sibelius and Sola. Now contains autograph changes by Sibelius in blue ink. It seems that the changes in the vocal lines to accommodate the English lyrics were made by Sola because the hand, ink, and even the music paper taped over m. 14 in No. 5 appear to be identical with the original manuscript (MS 113-48); 23pp.; shows a few changes in the English lyrics, originally typed, have been made in dark ink (see folios 14 & 17).

C-113-48d    Photostat (negative) of MS-113-48c after the vocal parts were altered to fit the English lyrics. Shows clearly m. 14 of No. 5 where the staff paper has been added to cover up the original vocal line. Also shows the rehearsal letters which were added faintly in pencil in the manuscript. Does not show any of Sibelius's "blue ink" additions nor any of the handwritten changes in text on folios 14 & 17. No title page; has 23 folios.

Placed in a large "Grand Lodge" envelope on which is written "November 1948" in the same hand as on the envelope for C 113-48b. A second hand has written "Sibelius/Publ. & Revised Versions."

C-113-48e

Galaxy's final version before the "1st Proof" was made. Contains autograph corrections by Sibelius in black crayon or pencil. Galaxy's corrections and additions appear in red pencil and green ink. 34pp. No title page, but at the bottom of the first page is typed the copyright notice with both the 1935 and the 1949 dates indicated. The "Finlandia Hymn" now appears on p. 34 as item No. 12. The chorale "The lofty Heav'n" is included (as it was in the 1936 edition), only this time there is a version for solo voice and organ along with that for TTBB chorus, both created by Kernochan. Also included is the TTBB arrangement of No. 6. This copy does not show the editorial additions by Sibelius in blue ink that appear in MS 113-48c. The changes in the text on pp 14 & 17 have been handwritten here. In other words, this is not a photostat of MS 113-48c. Note the change in pagination with the first page of music numbered as page 1 instead of page 2, as was done in the manuscript and other photostats.

C-113-48f

"1st Proof" sheets for 1950 edition prepared by Galaxy Music Corporation. Sent to Finland with editorial corrections by A. Walter Kramer (green ink) and Marshall Kernochan (dark blue ink), along with specific questions and comments for Sibelius written in the margins of the large sheets on which have been pasted the 8 1/2 x 11 pages of the score. Returned to Galaxy (possibly in August of 1949—see Consulate letter). Contains autograph corrections in black crayon or pencil by Sibelius. 34pp. Wrapping paper and label preserved at GLNY, which may have been used to ship the final proofs edited by Sibelius from Järvenpää. Size of the wrapping paper could have accommodated these sheets.

C-113-50    *Masonic Ritual Music*/by/Jean Sibelius/for/Male Voices/and/ Piano or Organ/Editing and English Texts/by Marshall Kernochan/Revised Edition, 1950/Issued for Masonic Use only/by/The Grand Lodge of Free and Accepted Masons/of the State of New York. The prefatory statement by Kernochan is dated January 1950. Contains 12 different musical pieces, of which two have TTBB versions prepared by Kernochan. Dedicated to Wäinö Sola. 34pp.

2.  Additional manuscript copies of opus 113 prepared by Sola with authorization from Sibelius were sent to the United States. One was sent to Iowa and is still extant. At least two other copies were sent but they have not been located.

MS-113-46ps    In 1946, Valter W. Granberg of the St. Henrick Lodge No. 5, Helsinki arranged for a "gift" manuscript to be sent to The Philalethes Society in care of the president, Walter A. Quincke, who resided in Los Angeles, CA. A letter acknowledging receipt of the manuscript in a bound volume and autographed by Sibelius is dated 11 December 1946 (see "Sibelius Family Collection 36/94," National Archives of Finland). At this writing, the Philalethes Society manuscript has not been located.

MS-113-48tn    In November 1948, Wäinö Sola made a duplicate of the manuscript he sent to Kernochan to prepare a second edition of opus 113. This manuscript was sent to Toivo Nekton, who lived in Hempstead, Long Island. There was, however, one important difference between MS-113-48 and MS-113-48tn: the Nekton manuscript had the original texts, whereas Kernochan's copy had none. At this writing, the Nekton manuscript has not been located.

MS-113-48io    Handwritten manuscript prepared by Wäinö Sola 15 December 1948 as a "gift" for the Grand Lodge of Iowa and preserved in the Iowa Masonic Library. Given in response to Harry L.

Haywood's request for something autographed by Sibelius for the Iowa Masonic Library. The manuscript carries Sibelius's signature on the title page. It contains 11 items and is copied from the same source used to produce MS 113-48. No lyrics included. The "Finlandia-Hymni," is once again included without a number and positioned on folio 17. For examples of how this manuscript differs from MS 113-48c, see: No. 2 (m. 13) where a tie makes clear the lowest note should be a B-flat; No. 1 has a title, "Avaushymni"; "Finlandia-Hymni" has "kuovolle 4.4.1938" written under "Jean Sibelius 1900"; "Ylistyshymni" has the whole note in m. 38 tied to the half note in m. 39.

3.  The preface to the 1936 edition, signed by the Grand Master of GLNY:

    This music is a tribute to Freemasonry by R∴W∴ Jean Sibelius of The Grand Lodge of Finland. How great an offering to the Fraternity this represents is obvious. We cannot say what the verdict of time may be, but the consensus of well-informed musical opinion is to the effect that Jean Sibelius is the foremost living composer, and is destined to take his place among the great masters of music.

    R∴W∴ Bro. Sibelius' music was inspired by his love for our ancient ritual, and those who have heard it are unanimous in ranking it with his best work. It was sent to the Grand Lodge of the State of New York, F. & A. M., in a true filial spirit, by its offspring, the Grand Lodge of Finland.

    In making this royal gift, the Grand Lodge of Finland requested that the music be used solely for Masonic purposes, and we shall use every endeavor to see that it reaches only duly accredited Masons who, we feel sure, will be only too glad to keep faith in this respect.

4.  In 1969 the Masons in Finland published *Rituaalimusiikki*, which represented their own version of opus 113 with texts in the Finnish language. The music in this edition represents the status of opus 113 *prior* to the preparation of MS-113-48 by Wäinö Sola in November 1948.

Eleven of the twelve numbers in C-113-50 constitute what the Masons in 1969 wanted to call Sibelius's opus 113. The twelfth item, "Finlandia-hymni," is set to a non-Masonic text by Sola and is not considered part of their ritual music. For this reason, this item appears in a supplement to the edition, along with four other pieces (one of which is by Sibelius), which have long been associated with Masonic activities but are not in any way related to opus 113.

The sequence of pieces in the 1969 edition of opus 113 is as follows (using the numbering found in the 1950 edition): 1 (1927); 1a (1948); 2 (1927); 2a (1927, in E major); 3 (1948 [pre-November 1948]); 9 (1946 [pre-November 1948]); 9a (same as no. 9 but in a lower key); 7 (1927/1948); 7a (same as 7 but in a lower key); 8 (1946 [pre-November 1948]); 8a (same as 8 but in a lower key); 4 (1927, [pre-November 1948]); 4a (Trio II in a lower key);10 (a version that does not exist in any of the extant documents which bear the stamp of Sibelius's approval: 1927, 1935, 1936, 1948 [Nov.], or 1950); 6 (a collation of the 1927 version, now in the key of F, with a later version, but not that of C-113-50); 6a (same as 6, but in a lower key); 11 (in a solo voice version that may be patterned after that which Kernochan provided for C-113-50); 5 (1927 and 1948 [the two different endings for the piece are printed one above the other]; 11a (same as 11 but in a lower key).

5.   English lyrics by Marshall Kernochan for *Masonic Ritual Music* (1950).

No. 2   Thoughts be our comfort in the days of darkness
        Thoughts that inspire the soul in joy or in pain
        Holy the fires ye light in souls benighted.
        Heavenly fires that gleam in the darkness of earth
        Shine in our souls and give us more light.

No. 3   Though young leaves be green at daybreak,
        Oft they die when day is done.
        Tender buds of hope and promise,
        Wither'd, yellow, they are gone.
        Yet such thoughts a man must conquer!

Pain and weakness they will bring.
Let him trust his heart for guidance!
Where, O Death, is then thy sting?

No. 4    Who ne'er hath blent his bread with tears,
Wakeful, despairing nights of sorrow,
Knowing no rest, nor hope, nor solace,
He knows thee not, O light of Heaven.

No. 5    How fair are Earth and Living!
How glorious are the heavens!
So praise the gifts celestial,
And cease from vain regret.
This night the stars are shining;
The welkin glows in beauty!
O Man! let thoughts as lofty
Bring hope and peace to thee through life.

No. 6    Onward, ye Brethren! strive for the Light!
The Light that the Lord hath given us for our Guide;
Who through murk and darkness of night
Hath led us in safety unto our reward.
Lo! how the fiery pillar is shining,
Lighting our steps when dark is the way.
And the Light of the World,
It cleaveth the gloomy blackness of night,
That else would engulf us!
Lo! the cloudy pillar, to shield us safe
When the sun would blister us.
Then forward where Faith revealeth the way!
For God is our Guide, and He will never fail!
Fires are gleaming, voices are singing,
Forth from Mount Neboh's heaven-storming height.
Salem! Salem!
Hark they call us upward and on to our Father's home.
Salem! Salem!

On the horizon, urging us onward, onward to God!
And His welcome is ringing forth from Mount Neboh:
"Come, all ye blest, to your Master's joy!" Salem!

No. 7    Whosoever hath a love of justice in his inmost heart,
Hath the seed of happiness, of a future of happiness in his soul.
He is victor in the last good fight.
God's own Light shall show him the Way,
Both now and ever, as of old.
Though rough and dark and thorny be the road,
Its perils shall not daunt him!
Gloriously shall he attain his journey's end;
Then, ah! then, by Jordan's waters he shall rest at last.

No. 8
v.1    Good and pleasant, O ye Brethren, 'tis to dwell in unity;
Strong to fight each others' battles, faithful to our mystic tie.
Precious is fraternal love, as the scent of flowers rare,
Myrrh and frankincense and spices with their fragrance fill the air.
Good and pleasant 'tis for Brethren to dwell in unity.

v.2    Keep we free from taint of slander, from the poisoned breath of spite;
Ever speaking words of kindness, gentle words of truth and light.
If a Brother stray or fall, Stretch we forth our helping hand;
Thus shall Masons ever prosper, Thus united shall they stand.
Good and pleasant 'tis for Brethren to dwell in unity.

No. 9    Praise Thy Holy Name on high! O Thou Architect Supreme!
Praise They Holy Name on high! O Thou Architect Supreme!
O God of God, O Light of Light, O Very God of Very God
Thou art the Father Omnipotent; Thine hands created the universe.
Thou art the Sum of Totality, Omnipotent!
O Architect of All. O Light of Light!

No. 11    The lofty Heav'n and widespread earth are singing Thy glory,
O Thou Architect of all!

As both were born by Word of Thine own speaking,
So into ashes Thou canst bid them fall.
The planets come and go at Thy commandment;
All living things exist by Thy creation.
Before Thy Holy Name we bow the knee.

No. 12

v.1 O gracious Lord, by whom the morning dawneth,
Now in Thy mercy bless our native land.
Let Thy Light shine, to drive away the shadows,
And free our homes from war's relentless hand.
To Thee our Brothers pray for truth and justice
And in Thy faith they firmly take their stand.

v.2 Thy wisdom infinite is our reliance;
Thy hand shall keep our people strong and free.
They sow the seed, they humbly wait the harvest,
And give Thee thanks, whatever it may be.
Our honest toil and zeal shall bring us gladness
For these are blessings, precious gifts from Thee.

6. Suggestions for use of *Masonic Ritual Music* at GLNY were provided when the manuscript was presented as a gift in 1935. A similar set of suggestions was also drawn up for the second edition. This latter set makes clear that the "Finlandia Hymn" is to be used ritually, "either at the opening or closing after prayer."

After the twelve pieces of the 1950 edition were listed, together with their suggested functions, the following general remarks were added:

These suggestions are based on the Standard New York work of which the Finnish work is originally a translation. It must be emphasized that they are merely suggestions and not in any way intended to limit the use of any of the numbers to prescribed places in the ritual.

The music is highly adaptable. Enterprising Masters, organists, and singers will find many other places where individual numbers will be found appropriate.

It is this adaptability which makes the music quite as practicable for other Grand Jurisdictions whose work differs from that of New York to a greater or lesser extent. It is merely a question of finding locally suitable places in their own work.

# DISCOGRAPHY
(1962–1996)

Numbers cited refer to those in the 1950 edition
of the *Masonic Ritual Music*

1962    Helsinki, Finland. Commission for the 40th anniversary of Suomi Lodge No. 1: Sept 1962, Matti Lehtinen (baritone) and Janne Raitio (organist). Finnish language. Nos. 1–8, 10. Decca SDLP 9007.

1965    Auckland, New Zealand. United Masters' Lodge of Research No. 167. English language. Nos. 1–12.

[1967]  Helsinki, Finland. Matti Lehtinen (baritone) and Janne Raitio (organist). English lyrics dubbed over the organ soundtrack of the 1962 recording cited above. Decca SDLP 9008.[1]

[1976]  Seattle, WA. King County Masonic Library: University of Washington Chorale, directed by Rodney Eichenberger with organist Gregory Vancil. Nos. 1–12.

1977    Helsinki, Finland. Matti Piipponen (baritone), Tauno Aikää (organist), and a double vocal quartet of Masonic members. Finnish Language. [See below for English language version, 1981.]

1979    Cologne, Germany. Grand Lodge of Germany, issued by "Forum Masonicum." German language. Nos. 1-12.

---

1    See Heineman, "Jean Sibelius," 8. Einari Marvia dates this recording in the year 1971.

1979    Helsinki, Finland. Live performance of an actual ritual performed in
        Suomi Lodge No. 1. Finnish language. Nos. 1–11 of opus 113, together
        with *Impromptu* (opus 5, no. 1) and *Intrada* (opus 111, no.1).

1981    Helsinki, Finland. English language version of the 1977 recording
        described above.

1992    Helsinki, Finland. CD issued by Suomi Lodge No. 1 in connection
        with the 1992 publication of the Finnish language edition of opus 113,
        edited by Einari Marvia et al. Nos. 1–11, together with *Impromptu*
        (opus 5, no. 1) and *Intrada* (opus 111, no.1).

1993    Espoo, Finland. *Musica Humana*. No. 5 (Anssi Hirvonen, tenor; Matti
        Vainio, organist); No. 6 (Heikki Siukola, tenor; Tauno Äikää, organist);
        No. 10 (Matti Vainio, organist). Finnish language. Recorded in The
        Old Church of Espoo. NECD 3581.

1994    Torino, Italy. CD issued together with Johann Freimauer's *A Journey
        Into a Masonic Lodge*. Italian language. Nos. 1–12.

1996    New York City, New York. GLNY issued a CD of live performances
        of Nos. 1–8 of both the 1927 version of opus 113 for voice (Martti
        Miettinen) and organ (Matti Hannula) and the 1940 Funtek version for
        voice (Martti Miettinen) and orchestra (The New York Metamorphoses
        Orchestra, cond. by Eugene Sirotkin) to commemorate the 130th
        anniversary of Sibelius's birth. Finnish language. The recording was
        also issued in a tape cassette format.

1996    Helsinki, Finland. *Works for Mixed Choir a cappella*. Includes the original
        verison of Sibelius's setting of all 3 verses of Jacob Tegengren's "Den
        höga himlen." Jubilate Choir, cond. by Astrid Riska. BIS–CD–825.

# *ABBREVIATIONS*

GLNY     Grand Lodge, F. & A. M., of the State of New York, 71 West 23rd Street, New York, NY 10010–4171.

KFC     Kernochan Family Collection (documents privately held by the heirs of the Marshall Kernochan and John Kernochan estates).

LML     The Chancellor Robert R. Livingston Masonic Library of Grand Lodge, 71 West 23rd Street, New York, NY 10010–4171. (Known prior to the mid-1980s as the Grand Lodge Library & Museum).

NFC     Nekton Family Collection (documents privately held by the heirs of the Toivo H. Nekton estate).

SFC     The Sjöblom Family Collection (documents privately held by the heirs of the George Sjöblom estate).

SSL     Suomi Suur-Loosi (Grand Lodge of Finland), Kasarmikatu 16 D, 00130 Helsinki 13, Finland.

# BIBLIOGRAPHY

"American Lodge of Research." *Masonic Outlook* (August-September 1935):12.

Anderson, James. *The Constitutions of the Free-Masons*. Philadelphia: Benjamin Franklin, 1734. Reprint: *Masonic Book Club*. Vol. 2. Bloomington, IL: Masonic Book Club, 1975.

*The ASCAP Biographical Dictionary of Composers, Authors, and Publishers*. Ed. by Daniel I. McNamara. New York: Thomas Y. Crowell, 1948.

*The ASCAP Biographical Dictionary*. 4th edition. New York: R. R. Bowker, 1980. S. v. "Huhn, Bruno."

"Behind the Scenes." *The New York Times* (24 Nov 1935):IX, 15.

Birch, Cyrilo, ed. *Anthology of Chinese Literature from Early Times to the Fourteenth Century*. New York: Grove Press, 1965–72.

Boyle, Nicholas. *Goethe, the Poet and the Age*. Vol. 1: 1749–1790. Oxford: Clarendon Press, 1991.

"A Brace of Festivals," *The New York Times* (23 April 1939):X, 7.

Calcott, Wellins. *A Candid Disquisition*. London: 1769. Reprint: *Universal Masonic Library*. Vol. 6. Lodgeton, KY: J. W. Leonard, 1856.

Carnes, Mark C. *Secret Ritual and Manhood in Victorian America*. New Haven: Yale University Press, 1989.

*Catalogue of Copyright Entries*. New Series. Vol. 30, no. 7, 1935: Part 3. Washington, DC: U.S. Government Printing Office.

*Catalogue of Copyright Entries*. New Series. Vol. 31, no.12, 1936: Part 3. Washington, DC: U.S. Government Printing Office.

*Catalogue of Copyright Entries*. New Series. Vol. 33, 1938: Part 3. Washington, DC: U.S. Government Printing Office.

Chailley, Jacques. *The Magic Flute, Masonic Opera*. Trans. by H. Weinstock. New York: Da Capo, 1971.

Dahlström. Fabian. *The Works of Jean Sibelius*. Helsinki:The Sibelius Society, 1987.

——. *Jean Sibelius: Thematisch-bibliographisches Verzeichnis seiner Werke.* Wiesbaden: Breitkopf & Härtel, 2003.

——. "Sibelius Research." In Glenda Goss, ed., *The Sibelius Companion.* Westport, CT: Greenwood Press, 1996, 297–315.

"Daniel Beard Gets Medal of Masons." *The New York Times* (5 May 1938):24.

Daniel, Oliver. *Stokowski, A Counterpoint of View.* New York: Dodd, Mead, 1982.

Denslow, Ray V. *Masonic Degrees.* [Trenton, MO?]: Published by the Author, 1928.

"Distinguished Visitors from Humanitas Masonic Club to be Presented in New York." *New Yorkin Uutiset* (23 Oct 1959):3.

Downes, Olin. "A Composer and His Nation." *The New York Times* (20 Dec 1939):IX, 7.

——. "Plight of Sibelius." *The New York Times* (2 July 1950):II, 6.

——. "Sibelius at Seventy." *The New York Times* (8 Dec 1935):22.

Dumenil, Lynn. *Freemasonry and American Culture 1880–1930.* Princeton: Princeton University Press, 1984.

Eastman, Luke. *Masonick Melodies.* Boston: T. Howe, 1818.

"80th Worcester Fete." *The New York Times* (1 Oct 1934):IX, 6.

Ekman, Karl. *Jean Sibelius: His Life and Personality.* Trans. by Edward Birse. 2nd ed. London: Alfred A. Knopf, 1938.

Ekman, Eero L. *Highlights of Masonic Life in Nordic Countries.* Turku: Turun Sanomat Oy, 1993.

"Finland Observes Sibelius's Birthday." *The New York Times* (9 Dec 1935):26.

"Finland Salutes US in Broadcast." *The New York Times* (2 Jan 1939):2.

"Finland's Voice." *The New York Times* (2 Jan 1939):22.

"500,000 Visit Fair at Music Festival." *The New York Times* (2 May 1938):1, 19.

Forke, Alfred. *Blüthen Chinesischer Dichtung.* Magdeburg: Faber, 1899.

"Freemasonry and Religion." Masonic Information Center (Dec 1993).

Freimauer, Johann. *A Journey into a Masonic Lodge.* Torino: 1994.

Gerrard, J. G. "Karamzin, Mme de Stael, and the Russian Romantics." *American Contributions to the Seventh International Congress of Slavists (Warsaw, August 21–27, 1973).* II, 221–46.

"Germany Gains Listed by Hitler." *The New York Times* (2 May 1938):3.

Gilman, Lawrence. "Sibelius in America." *The New York Herald Tribune* (6 December 1936).

Godwin, Joscelyn. "Layers of Meaning in the *Magic Flute*." *Musical Quarterly* 65 (Oct 1979): 471–92.

Gold, Edith. "Would Ban 'Finlandia' Now." *The New York Times* (20 Oct 1942):20.

Goss, Glenda Dawn. *Jean Sibelius and Olin Downes*. Boston: Northeastern University Press, 1995.

———, ed. *The Sibelius Companion*. Westport, CT: Greenwood Press, 1996.

"Grand Lodge of Finland." *Masonic Outlook* (March 1925):138.

Hamill, J. H. "Vocal Music in Craft Ceremonies and After Proceedings." *Ars Quatuor Coronatorum* 88 (1976):187–89.

Haunch, T. O. "The Dedication of Freemasons' Hall 23 May 1776." *Ars Quatuor Coronatorum* 88 (1976):179-81.

Heineman, Jean O. "Jean Sibelius." *Knight Templar* (Dec 1980):7–10.

———. "Recorded Masonic Music" *Knight Templar* (Feb 1980):23–4.

"Hitler Awards Medeal to Composer." *The New York Times* (9 Dec 1935):26.

"Homage to a Master." *Musical America* (10 Dec 1935):5–6.

Johnson, Harold E. *Sibelius*. New York: Alfred A. Knopf, 1959.

Karttunen, Antero. "True and False *Andante Festivo*." *Finnish Music Quarterly* (4/95):57–8.

Kernochan, Marshall. "Craft Music on Program for Lodge of Research." *Masonic Outlook* (April 1940): 151.

———. "*Masonic Ritual Music* by Sibelius." *Masonic Outlook* (May 1937):178.

———. "Sibelius' Masonic Ritual Music." *Masonic Family Magazine* (March-April 1950):14–15.

Kilpiläinen, Kari. *The Jean Sibelius Manuscripts at Helsinki University. A Complete Catalogue.* Wiesbaden: Breitkopf & Härtel, 1991.

———. "Sibelius Eight. What Happened to It?" *Finnish Music Quarterly* (4/1995):30–5.

Klinge, Matti. *A Brief History of Finland.* Keuruu: Otava, 1990.

Landon, H. C. Robbins. *Mozart and the Masons*. New York: Thames & Hudson, 1991.

Lipson, Dorothy Ann. "The Americanization of Freemasonry." *Freemasonry in Federalist Connecticut*. Princeton: Princeton University Press, 1977, 46–62.

Lönnrot, Elias. *Kalevala. The Land of Heroes.* 2 vols. Trans. by W.F. Kirby. New York: Dutton, 1974.

Macoy, Robert. *Worshipful Master's Assistant*. New York: Macoy Publishing and Masonic Supply, 1885/1947.

Mair, Victor H., ed. *The Columbia Anthology of Traditional Chinese Literature.* New York: Columbia University Press, 1994.

Marvia, Einari. *Sibeliuksen Rituaalimusiikki.* Acta Minervae III. Helsinki: Tutkimusloosi Minerva No. 27, 1984.

———. "Sibeliuksen Rituaalimusiikki." *Näkymättömän Temppelin Rakentajat.* Helsinki: Otava, 1994, 227–44.

[Marvia, Einari.] "The Ritual Music of Sibelius." [Typescript available at SSL.]

"Masonic Symphony Plays." *The New York Times* (13 April 1953):31.

McLeod, Wallace. "Wellins Calcott, and His List of the Officers of Lodges and Provincial Grand Lodges, 1772." *Transactions: The American Lodge of Research* 16 (March 1986-December 1986):83–100.

*Monitor of the Work, Lectures and Ceremonies of Ancient Craft Masonry in the Jurisdiction of the Grand Lodge of New York.* New York: Grand Lodge of the State of New York, 1904.

"Music." *The New York Times* (27 Dec 1926):20.

"Music at Grand Lodge." *Masonic Outlook* (June-July 1937):198.

Naumann, Johann Gottlieb. *Two Masonic Pieces.* Ed. by John Morehen. New York: Oxford University Press, 1979.

Nekton, Toivo, H. "Highlights in the History of American Freemasonry in Finland 1922–1949." *Transactions: The American Lodge of Research* 6 (July 1952-December 1953):22–33.

———. *Morton Lodge No. 63 F. & A. M.: Its History 1797–1947.* Hempstead, NY: Morton Lodge, 1949.

*The New Grove Dictionary of American Music.* Ed. by H. Wiley Hitchcock and Stanley Sadie. 4 vols. London: Macmillan, 1986.

*The New Grove Dictionary of Instruments.* Ed. by Stanley Sadie. 3 vols. London: Macmillan, 1984.

*The New Grove Dictionary of Music and Musicians.* Ed. by Stanley Sadie. 20 vols. London: MacMillan,1980.

"News of the Week in Review." *The New York Times* (24 Dec 1939):IV, 1.

"1,000,000 Watch Preview Parade." *The New York Times* (1 May 1938):I, 35.

Ostman, Emil L., and Willy W. Rutzy. "25 Years of Finlandia Masonic Club." Privately printed ca. 1980. 4pp. [Copy in SFC]

"Philharmonic Severs Red Tape of War to Assist Jan Sibelius."*The New York Times* (7 April 1945):17.

"Plight of Sibelius Confuses Capital." *The New York Times* (10 July 1950):16.

Pollack, Thomas G. *Ivanhoe Masonic Quartettes*. New York: Wm. A Dodd, 1867.

Pratt, Harry Rogers. "Hardy Finland Speaks Through Sibelius." *The New York Times Magazine* (8 Dec 1935):10, 16.

Preston, William. *Illustrations of Masonry*. 2nd ed. London: 1775. Reprint: Vol. 4, *Masonic Book Club*. Bloomington, IL: Masonic Book Club, 1973.

Price, Carl F., ed. *Sing … Brothers, Sing*. New York: Gettinger Printing, 1940.

*Proceedings of the Grand Lodge of New York* (1935, 1938).

Reinecke, Carl, ed. *Mozarts Kompositionen für Freimaurer*. Leipzig: Breitkopf & Härtel, [ca. 1910].

Reinikainen, Paavo. "Masonic Ritual Music in Finland." Helsinki: Grand Lodge of Finland, n.d. [pamphlet]

Rossel, Sven H. *A History of Scandinavian Literature 1870–1980*. Trans. by Anne C. Ulmer. Minneapolis, MN: University of Minnesota Press, 1982.

Schober, Franz von. *Gedichte*. 2nd ed. Leipzig: Weber, 1865.

Schuler, Heinz. "Mozarts Maurerische Trauermusik KV447/479a: Eine Dokumentation." *Mitteilungen der Internationalen Stiftung Mozarteum* 40 (1992):46–70.

Sharp, Arthur. "Masonic Songs and Song Books of the Late XVIII Century." *Ars Quatuor Coronatorum* (1952):84–95.

———. "Sibelius' Masonic Ritual Music." *Ars Quatuor Coronatorum* 75 (1962):1–8.

Sibelius, Jean. *Kasikirjoituksi*. Manuscripts (facsimiles) from Archives of Oy R. E. Westerlund Ab. Ed. by Lauri Solanterä. Finnish text by Eino Roiha; Swedish text by Erik Bergman; English text by Paul Sjöblom. Helsingfors, Westerlund, 1945.

"Sibelius … Composer … Freemason." *Empire State Mason* 5 ("Holiday Issue" 1957):18.

"Sibelius's Death Denied." *The New York Times* (2 Dec 1939):3.

"Sibelius Is Safe at Finnish Forest Home." *The New York Times* (3 Dec 1939):52.

"Sibelius Sends Message." *The New York Times* (20 Dec 1939):5.

Sjöblom, Paul. "Finlandia as a Song and the Contribution of George Sjöblom." *Finnish American Horizons* (1976):257–65.

———. "How Sibelius Came to Smoke the Same Cigar with Me," *Suomen Silta* (3/95):20–21.

———. "An Interview of Sibelius." *Musical America* 50 (10 Dec 1940):11, 34.

Sjöblom, Yrjö [George]. "Finlandia lauluna." *Suomen Kuvalehti* (8 Dec 1945):1258–59.

———. "Homage for Sibelius on His 70th Birthday." *Musical America* (10 Dec 1935):3, 5–6.

Smith, Douglas. "Freemasonry and the Public in Eighteenth-Century Russia." *Eighteenth-Century Studies* 29 (Fall, 1995):25-44.

Smyth, Frederick. "Recorded Music." *Transactions of Quatuor Coronati Lodge* 88 (1976):108–10.

Sola, Wäinö. "Jean Sibelius as a Composer of Freemason Music." *California Freemason* (1958):44–5. [This article, written in English, first appeared in the memorial issue of *Kaukoputki*, the official publication of the Grand Lodge of Finland.]

——. "Jean Sibelius vapanmuurari musiikin säveltäjänä." *Koilliskulma* (1955):4-6. Reprinted in *Koilliskulma* (May 1997y):66–7.

"Stated Communication for 30 September 1935." *Transactions: The American Lodge of Research* 11 (Feb 1935-Sept 1935):23.

"Stated Communication for 29 November 1949." *Transactions: American Lodge of Research* 5 (May 1949-April 1951):196.

"Stated Communication for 29 April 1952." *Transactions: American Lodge of Research* 5 (April 1951-January 1952):312.

Stoeckel, Carl. "Some Recollections of the Visit of Sibelius to America in 1914." *Scandinavian Studies* (1971):53-88.

"Stokowski Leads at Dix." *The New York Times* (11 Dec 1941):38.

Stork, Charles Wharton, trans. *Anthology of Swedish Lyrics from 1750 to 1925*. New York: American Scandinavian Foundation, 1930.

Straus, Noel. "Sibelius Score. The Story of His 'Masonic Ritual Music' Told for the First Time." *The New York Times* (3 Oct 1948):II, 7.

"Symphony in Wood of Finns Has Debut." *The New York Times* (5 May 1939):18.

Tawaststjerna, Erik. *Jean Sibelius*. 5 vols. [in Finnish] Helsinki: Otava, 1965–88.

——. *Jean Sibelius*. 3 vols. [in Swedish] Helsinki: Söderström, 1991–93.

——. *Sibelius, 1865–1905*. Vol. 1. Trans. by Robert Layton. Berkeley & Los Angeles: University of California Press, 1976.

——. *Sibelius, 1904–1914*. Vol. 2. Trans. by Robert Layton. Berkeley & Los Angeles: University of California Press, 1986.

——. *Sibelius*. Vol. 3. *Trans. by Robert Layton*. London: Faber & Faber, 1997.

Terrell, Gisela Schlüter. *The Harold E. Johnson Jean Sibelius Collection at Butler University. A Complete Catalogue*. Indianapolis, IN: Butler University, 1993.

Town, Salem. *A System of Speculative Masonry*. Salem, NY: Dodd & Stevenson, 1818.

Vinton, David, ed. *Masonick Minstrel*. Dedham, MA: Herman Mann, 1816.

Voipio, Anni. "Sibelius as His Wife Sees Him." *The New York Times* (28 Jan 1940):II, 8.

Webb, Thomas Smith. *The Freemason's Monitor.* New ed. Salem, MA: Cushing & Appleton, 1812.

Wigmore, Richard, trans. *Schubert: The Complete Song Texts.* New York: Schirmer Books, 1988.

Williams, Hermine W. "George (Yrjö) Sjöblom: Jean Sibelius's Link with America." (forthcoming)

Wood, Ralph. "The Miscellaneous Orchestral and Theatre Music." In *The Music of Sibelius.* Ed. by Gerald Abraham. New York: W. W. Norton, 1947, 38-90.

"World's Fair Festival Today." *The New York Times* (1 May 1938):X, 5.

"Yale Glee Singers Visit Sibelius in Helsingfors." *The New York Times* (9 July 1939):21.

# INDEX

978-0-595-50088-8
0-595-50088-9

Lightning Source UK Ltd.
Milton Keynes UK
14 February 2011

167503UK00002B/146/P

9 780595 500888